FrameBreaking Leadership Development

Think differently about work experiences

to achieve more, faster.

FrameBreaking
Leadership Development

*Think differently
about work experiences
to achieve more, faster.*

Mark Kizilos, Ph.D.

**EXPERIENCE-BASED DEVELOPMENT
ASSOCIATES, LLC**
Chanhassen, MN

FrameBreaking™ Leadership Development

Think differently about work experiences to achieve more, faster.

Ordering Information

Quantity sales. Special discounts are available for quantity purchases by organizations, trade associations, coaches, and others. Contact the publisher for details.

Individual sales. FrameBreaking Leadership Development is available online through the e-store at FrameBreaking.com as well as Amazon.com.

ISBN-13: 978-0984922208
ISBN-10: 0984922202

Book Website
www.FrameBreaking.com
Email: info@FrameBreaking.com

Give feedback on the book at:
feedback@FrameBreaking.com

Printed in U.S.A.

*To Olivia and Alex, in the hope that they will one day
expertly navigate their own professional careers;
To Melissa, whose contributions have been woven into this
book in numerous ways;
And to my parents, Betty and Tolly, who have been there for
me through all manner of experience.*

Contents

Figures

Acknowledgements

I have developed the ideas in this book over the last twenty years by reflecting on my own experiences as a professor, consultant, and corporate executive. I am especially thankful to the clients I have worked with who were interested in pushing the envelope and creating new best practices for experience-based development. Without the opportunity to work intensively with leaders from these companies, I would never have had the experiences I needed to create this book.

In addition to the insights I developed from consulting for some of the world's top companies, I have learned a great deal from working beside great leaders and thinkers. I owe special thanks to David Hatch, founder of the Center for Leadership Solutions. He first hired me as an intern at PepsiCo and later introduced me to the concept of experience-based development. He has provided invaluable mentorship throughout my career, and I evolved many of the ideas presented in this book in reflecting on our animated conversations about leadership development.

Also, thanks to Morgan McCall. Even though Morgan's office at the University of Southern California was just down the hall from my Ph.D. student office, I have had only limited opportunity to work directly with him. But, the few opportunities that I had to learn from him have made a significant impact on my thinking about the role of experiences in development. The example of Jerry's Story in Chapter 2 was based in part on a story I heard from Morgan.

I also owe special thanks to two great leaders with whom I have worked closely over the years: Charlie Feld, when he was CIO of Delta Air Lines, and Dick Harrington, when he was CEO of the Thomson Corporation (now Thomson Reuters). These two leaders provided me with invaluable opportunities to do good work and learn from my own experiences while focused on developing leadership capability in others.

I would also like to express gratitude for some of the professional mentors and colleagues who have encouraged my interests in experience-based development. Jim Smith, Bob Bogart, and Pam Kushmerick were three great bosses who supported my work, and, I must thank several colleagues for their contributions at various points along the way—Paul Bly, Kimberly Bates McCarl, John Haleblian, Ben Porter, and Tim Donahue.

Preface

As I began to write this book, I looked back on my own developmental experiences for insight and to test the tools that I was creating. Perhaps the most striking insight for me was realizing how my personal approach to learning and development has been shaped by my early life experiences. I was raised by a mother who was a physicist, and a father who was an organization development professional. While my mother typically left her work at the office, my father brought his personal passion for human development home from work every day. His intentional approach to learning had a significant impact on how he and my mother raised me and my brothers.

This was a house in which we set goals for academic excellence, our progress was monitored, and we got regular feedback. As early as middle school, my grade point average was plotted on a chart next to those of my two older brothers. We had performance appraisal discussions at the end of each quarter to review recent performance and discuss what would be needed to achieve our goals in the next quarter—perhaps a little less time watching Gilligan's Island and a few more evening sessions with dad to review math problems.

The value of reflecting on my experience—not just from an achievement perspective, but from a learning perspective—was a key lesson embedded in much of my upbringing.

When I was preparing my college applications, I remember my dad helping me to put my experiences into a broader context to understand what I had learned from some of the things that I had done. For example, when I was in the ninth grade, I became obsessed with laser holograms. Three-dimensional laser holography was pretty new at the time (it still hasn't made its way into most homes), and the idea of creating a three-dimensional picture of an object with a laser seemed like magic. When I found a book that provided a set of plans for building a holography table that would enable me to make my own holograms, I became obsessed with making it as a school science project.

This was 1978, and there were many challenges I would need to overcome: without the Internet, even tracking down the necessary supplies was a challenge. I began by contacting the high school physics teacher, who I thought might be a valuable resource. He told me about a high school senior who had tried such a project and failed. Undeterred, I pressed on, and he ultimately agreed to provide me with my own private room to work in at the high school—and he agreed to give me access to a laser.

It took several months of labor to fabricate a 100+ pound steel-topped table and a set of specialized fixtures, but I eventually began attempting to create holograms. After much trial and error, I realized that I needed to convince the high school custodian to turn off the ventilation system while I was working because the vibrations were too disruptive to my sensitive equipment. To get a good image, I needed the holography table to be stable to within one quarter of a wavelength of light for a full 30 seconds. Once he agreed to turn off the ventilation system, I had my first success. I successfully created a hologram of a white chess king.

I was thrilled, and the accomplishment ended up getting me on the local evening news as a kid with great prospects in science. However, I had no interest in science. In fact, when I got to high school the next year, I didn't even take physics. I simply had a vision for something that I wanted to create and was willing to do whatever was necessary to realize that vision.

My father helped me to see that what I had learned was more about leadership than science. I had orchestrated a complex project that involved securing diverse resources, enlisting the efforts of others, and overcoming a range of non-technical challenges. The learning was much broader than learning about holography. I had learned:

- *Researching—Gathering and synthesizing information from diverse sources*

- *Influencing—Gaining support of the physics teacher and help of the custodian*

- *Persevering—Sustaining motivation over a long period to achieve a significant outcome*

- *Promoting—Spotting a media opportunity and making connections to get publicity*

Breaking down my experience in this way helped me to see that I was actually learning a lot more than I had realized.

This idea has stuck with me throughout my career, and it has helped me to get more out of the experiences that I have had along the way. It also helped me to think differently about developing others.

As a consultant, some of the more interesting work my colleagues and I did involved documenting the developmental experiences of successful leaders. After we interviewed a number of the 101 leaders whose career stories provided the foundation for this book, I had a flash of insight. I realized that, until we spoke, many of the people I was interviewing had never *processed* their experiences in the way that had become second nature to me. For most, identifying the key developmental experiences from their career was easy. These experiences stood out in their minds because they usually involved the biggest challenges or most stressful situations that they had encountered. But pointing to the specific learning that they had gained out of those experiences was much more challenging. For many, even some of the most successful leaders, there was a long pause after I asked them to tell me about what they had learned. A common response was simply "Hmmm… that's a tough question."

Only about ten or fifteen percent of the leaders with whom I spoke were able to quickly articulate the lessons they had taken away from their most developmental experiences. These tended to be the most successful of all the leaders with whom I spoke. They quickly recited not only the key lessons that they had gleaned from their experiences, but they could point to specific instances when they applied these lessons to subsequent challenges.

Clearly, all the leaders I spoke with had learned a great deal from experiences throughout their careers. Many were successful CEOs, executive vice presidents, and function or department leaders. But in the absence of a clear framework, language, and set of tools for thinking about their experience, they were at a loss for words to relate what they had learned.

I couldn't help but think that, despite their success, they were leaving valuable insights unleveraged. When we explored their experiences together and I helped them to identify what they had learned, my suspicions were confirmed. I guided these leaders through a simple thought process and they began to see patterns in their own behavior—successes and failures—that they had not seen previously. *They were extracting the learning from experiences that they had five, ten, or even twenty years in the past!*

Research has shown that when you remain unaware of what you have learned, you are less likely to apply it in new situations (Büssing and Herbig, 2003). Without explicitly going through a thought process to articulate your learning and fit it into your existing knowledge structures, the insight or capability that you develop tends to be trapped in the context in which you learned it. Psychologists and learning theorists have long labeled this the "inert knowledge problem" (Whitehead, 1929). Your insights tend to become tightly glued to the specifics of the situation, making it difficult to draw on the learning when you encounter different situations where the learning might be applied to improve your performance (Gentner et al. 2009).

Yet, it is only your ability to *apply* your insights and knowledge to new situations that enables you to effectively take on larger responsibilities and make a bigger contribution. It would have been easy for me, for example, to associate all of my learning from the holography project with the specifics of the situation—overcoming the technical challenges associated with creating a nifty science project. But realizing the broader leadership capabilities that I had been developing gave me confidence and helped me to see ways I could apply those lessons in new situations to tackle different challenges. In fact, the essential dynamics of that early experience have shaped the main theme of my career: being driven by the desire to realize a personal vision for some significant achievement and mustering whatever resources are needed to achieve it.

This fundamental insight sparked an idea that became the driving force behind this book: to create a simple, easy-to-use framework and set of tools to help people learn more effectively from their experiences and apply those lessons to future challenges.

Take charge of your own development

Individuals are increasingly asked to "take charge" of their own development. While some may see this trend cynically, as a convenient justification for decreasing organizational investment in people, I see it as a simple reality of our times. Here is how one highly successful leader in the financial services industry put it to me:

> *I think in big companies we often forget that your development is really 95 percent in your own hands. You've got to be very proactive about where you're headed, and why, and what you want your bosses and their bosses to do to help you.*

Taking charge of your own development is an essential survival skill for the modern workplace. Organizations have become less paternalistic, and employees are no longer guaranteed a career with one company. Moreover, in many industries, things are simply changing too rapidly for organizations to reliably look into the future to provide guidance regarding an efficient career path.

Rather than waiting for someone to point out a clear path for your career, you are better off "grabbing a machete" and clearing your own path. The ability to make your own success is itself a key leadership competency. It is your capability, rather than your tenure, that will guarantee success whatever you do and wherever you do it.

While organizations may be earnestly seeking to empower their people to take charge of their own careers, they have not had a robust set of tools to do the job. What can aspiring leaders do to forward their careers? Which experiences will provide valuable lessons? Which experiences may lead to derailment? This book and the tools available online at FrameBreaking.com can help with these and other key questions.

Shakespeare wrote "All the world's a stage, and all the men and women merely players." In the context of the modern work world, we might reword this to say, "All the world's a classroom, and all the men and women merely students." Heightening awareness of experience-based development should act as a catalyst for you to re-envision your current work with an enhanced Learning Mindset.

Audience for this book

This book is written for leaders and aspiring leaders. It will be most valuable to you if:

1) You are already a leader, but seek to advance to the next level of success in your career.

2) You are not yet a leader, but seek to prepare yourself for a leadership position.

3) You are responsible for the development of others in your organization, either as a manager, or as a human resources, leadership development, talent management, or coaching professional.

While I believe that the underlying concepts I introduce in this book are relevant for anyone working in an organization, the central purpose of this book is to assist those who aspire to greater leadership success. Because this is my focus, the quotations that I include throughout the book are all from leaders. I have disguised the names and companies of those I have quoted, and I have altered some of their words to ensure their anonymity, but they all provide a similar perspective— that of the successful leader reflecting on their path to success.

A Field Guide to *FrameBreaking*

Chapter 1 explains why experience-based development is critical for leaders. The leadership talent within an organization is segmented into three broad groups: the bottom, which consists of those individuals who are under-performing and need to focus on "getting in the game"; the middle, which consists of those individuals who are performing at or near standard, but who need to focus on "improving their game"; and the top talent group, which consists of the current and next generation of leaders who need to focus on "changing the game" or "playing a different game." The competencies most critical for those trying to change the game are higher-order competencies, such as judgment, insight, and perspective. These can only be learned from experience.

Chapter 2 introduces the concept of a "contribution trajectory" to describe the careers of successful leaders. I argue that the best leaders operate on a steeper contribution trajectory than others. The best leaders are able to attain a steep trajectory because of their ability to learn from their experiences and leverage that learning to take on challenges of increasing magnitude over time. This ability distinguishes them from other leaders and builds their critical higher-order competencies.

I present three foundational principles for understanding the process by which leaders develop through experience. These principles are so basic that they often go unstated. However, since the current state of practice does not sufficiently leverage these principles to drive more effective leadership development, I believe it is worth stating them explicitly:

1) Successful leaders are shaped by the experiences they have throughout their lives.

2) Any experience can be developmental, but some work experiences will be predictably more developmental for *you* than others.

3) Experience will only accelerate development if useful lessons are learned from it and are applied appropriately in new situations.

The key implications from these simple principles for your development as a leader are:

1) The experiences you have in your professional life make a difference in how you develop;

2) What you get out of an experience will depend upon your capabilities and preparation going into it;

3) And if you don't bring a Learning Mindset to your experience, you won't accelerate your development, even if you have "great experiences."

Chapter 3 presents the FrameBreaking Leadership Development Model. The model provides a lens for evaluating the developmental value of any experience by assessing the extent of Intensity and Stretch that it presents. By combining the two dimensions together, four distinct types of experience are described: Delivering, Mastering, Broadening, and FrameBreaking.

Chapters 4 through 7 describe each of the four experience types in greater detail and provide a set of questions for exploring the potential value of various types of experiences. These chapters will be most valuable if you are seeking to make a difference in your own career or the career of someone you are helping to develop.

Chapter 8 closes with a few words about self development. This is included as encouragement for those who are about to embark on the implementation of their own experience-based development plan.

The final section of the book, **Resources Available from FrameBreaking.com,** provides a brief overview of the resources that are available to help you apply the FrameBreaking

Leadership Development Process and tools to achieve greater success in your own career.

1

___

Why Learning from Experience is the Key to Becoming a Successful Leader

"A man who carries a cat by the tail learns something he can learn in no other way."

- Mark Twain

Early in my career I became interested in what I saw as a perplexing disconnect between how leaders *naturally* develop and how organizations go about trying to *formally* develop them.

As we all do, leaders develop through a combination of experiences, relationships, and formal learning. In recent years, some have described the mix among these different learning modes using the expression "70-20-10" as shorthand to say that on-the-job experience accounts for 70% of the learning that leaders need to be effective, relationships account for 20%, and formal learning (which consists of training, books, and the like) accounts for just 10% (McCall et al. 1988; Lindsey, Homes, and McCall, 1987).

While some may debate the precision of the 70-20-10 formulation, many organizations have adopted it as a learning philosophy to emphasize experience-based and social learning over formal approaches (McCall, 2010). Despite the widespread adoption of the learning philosophy, the impact of 70-20-10 on the effectiveness of organizational learning practice has been minimal. The primary reason is that 70-20-10 does not provide concrete guidance for developing better leaders. In a way, it simply expands on the old saying, "Experience is the best teacher."

That said, even if the only contribution of the 70-20-10 formulation was to focus our attention on learning from on-the-job experience, it would represent an important contribution. Raising awareness that people learn in diverse ways is a contribution because the intuitive model for workplace learning that most people carry around in their heads equates all professional development with formal learning.

That the traditional learning paradigm dominates professional practice is evident by looking at how organizations attempt to develop leaders. The standard approaches—classroom lectures, leader-led discussions, case studies, books, articles, e-learning programs—all employ a formal learning model, where an "expert" acts as a guide in conveying to others the "important things to learn" in some knowledge or skill area. The expert creates a "map of the terrain" and attempts to orient others to that map. The formal learning model often involves a type of *mediated* learning, because it focuses on an expert who acts as a mediator between the person who wants to learn and the subject that they are trying to learn. Because the mediator is an expert in the subject at hand, he or she should, the reasoning goes, be able to help the individual wrestle with new concepts and avoid fruitless digressions.

This formal, mediated model of learning is so deeply ingrained, in part, because by the time we start our professional careers, most of us have spent upwards of fifteen of our formative years learning within a formal educational system. It is also ubiquitous because it has a large sweet spot: any situation where one's performance can be enhanced by learning from best practices rationally codified by someone else. Another reason for the ubiquity of the mediated learning model is that it provides a compelling tool for busy managers operating with a "quick-fix" mentality. If an employee needs to build communication skills, sending him or her to a communications class presents a simple and manageable solution. Whether the prescribed training effectively changes behavior is a separate, often ignored, question.

While a broad range of knowledge, skills, and abilities fall into this sweet spot, not everything does. Different capabilities are critical for those individuals attempting to make a significantly larger contribution to the organization than they have to date or create a path to success in an area where no clear path exists. These individuals need to develop capabilities that enable them to operate at a higher level, on a bigger playing field, with higher stakes. They need to learn how to handle novel situations in which it is not practical, or even desirable, to mimic the approaches of others who may be generally acknowledged as "experts."

The capabilities needed to effectively lead on a larger playing field require learning not from the best practices codified by others, but from best practices derived from one's own experiences.

Developing top talent requires a different focus

Figure 1 depicts a distribution curve that represents the expected distribution of talent within any large organization. Most of an organization's people are clustered in the middle of the curve—either just below the average or just above the average—and there are small tails of underperforming and highly talented individuals.

The curve is divided into three broad talent segments, and the development needs and appropriate approach to learning vary across the segments. As will be shown in the following pages, the experience-based development approach that is the subject of this book is particularly critical for those in the top talent segment.

"Getting in the game"

The left side of the curve shows those employees who are in some way not making the grade. They need to improve their skills just to stay in the game. While I describe the development appropriate for this level as "Remedial Training," most

Figure 1.

The best leaders need to work on "Changing the game"

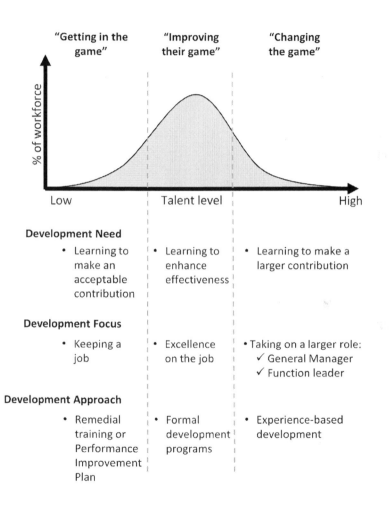

organizations do not invest much in the development of those in this segment. The skill levels and knowledge required for acceptable performance are clearly understood and measurable, but these individuals have demonstrated a level of competence that falls short of established standards. As a result, these individuals are viewed as underperforming.

Instead of investing in training, the typical organizational approach to this segment is to use performance improvement plans to manage these individuals out of the organization. This advice was spelled out by Jack Welch of General Electric as his own 20-70-10 technique (Welch and Byrne, 2001). Welch would sort individuals into Good, Average, and Poor categories and manage out the Poor (the "10"). While this approach to the bottom segment has come under fire over the years (McGregor, 2006), the point here is that the bottom talent segment is typically viewed as a problem to be managed, and only crude tools are employed to manage it.

"Improving their game"

This segment comprises the vast majority of the workforce. It includes both the organization's solid performers and those who are on their way to becoming solid performers. I recall the wise words of one CEO regarding the performance enhancement segment when we were discussing his organization's leadership development approach: "I want to develop strong talent at every level of the organization—not just at the top."

This CEO was telling me that he wanted to be sure that the company's approach did not send the message that only rapid advancement was valued. To the contrary, he wanted to have lots of engaged people in this middle segment— people capable of making significant contributions where they were and content to make those contributions in a mid-level position. He was adamant that the organizational message to those in this talent segment needed to be, "We value you and want to help you to succeed and achieve a greater level of excellence."

Those in this segment can benefit greatly from the standard leadership development approaches that most organizations offer: classroom learning, competency assessments, e-learning programs, and all manner of programs and approaches to improve work-related skills. All these methods offer precisely the types of skill-building that people in this segment need to help them with "improving their game."

"Changing the game"

The current and next generations of the most successful leaders reside in the top talent segment. Whether they are aspiring to take on their first significant leadership role or move into a larger leadership role, these individuals need a different type of development. While some may also need targeted knowledge or skill development from time to time ("rounding off the sharp edges" is a phrase I have heard frequently about hard-driving top talent leaders), their challenges are not typically related to skill deficiencies or incremental improvement. These individuals proactively address such problems when they become aware of them or they have already taken advantage of the available formal learning opportunities.

So, the focus in this top talent segment needs to be on developing the ability to make a significantly larger contribution than they are already making. If those in the performance enhancement segment are trying to "improve their game," those in the top talent segment are trying to "change the game" or "play a different game." This most typically involves building perspective, enhancing the ability to make significant business judgments, and developing awareness and insight. These higher-order capabilities are what enable the leader, for example, to get things done across a complex and far-flung enterprise, to deal with tough competitors, or to determine the best direction to take the company's product portfolio over the next five years.

These higher-order capabilities can only be effectively developed through experience. If one were to ask for a class on "perspective," it would be almost as ludicrous as when the food critic Anton Ego (in the Disney Pixar animated movie, Ratatouille)asks for "a plate of fresh perspective." How do you make that?

The most important leadership qualities can only be developed through experience

Leaders intuitively realize that the key capabilities for success are not developed in a classroom (McCall, 2010). When they describe how they have learned throughout their careers, they tend to paint a picture of learning that looks a lot like 70-20-10. Namely, they point to real work experience as having played the most significant role in their own development, followed by learning from others, and only occasionally mentioning formal learning as important. When asked directly, they will acknowledge that the formal learning experiences they have had throughout their career—a college degree, an MBA, a company-sponsored training program—were helpful, but they tend to attribute their success to having had critical real world experiences.

This is because leaders view their experience as developing the capabilities they value the most—higher-order leadership capabilities along with foundational values, such as persistence and a strong work ethic. Other abilities that they acquire from formal learning experiences may contribute to their success, but they are not as highly valued because they are *baseline* skills. That is, they are necessary but not sufficient—while one needs theses skills for success, they do not differentiate the "best" leaders from the "rest" of the pack. Generally, knowledge available through formal means is widely available, and as such becomes *commoditized*.

Figure 2 plots a few illustrative leadership competencies along two dimensions to make the point that the most critical leadership qualities are developed through experience. The dimensions on the 2x2 matrix reflect two key questions that can be used to think about any leadership competency:

1) Can the competency be acquired from formal learning or only from experience?

2) Is the competency something that differentiates top performers from others, or is it considered a baseline competency that is required simply to be in a leadership role?

Figure 2.
Differentiating competencies of the best leaders and how they are developed

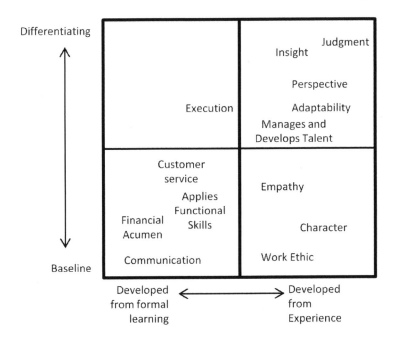

The competencies on the left side of Figure 2 are those that can be learned from formal learning approaches—they are trainable. While they may be critically important for the organization, they tend not to *differentiate the best* leaders from the rest. Those who have not yet mastered a competency on the left side of this figure and wish to be successful leaders would be well advised to take a class, read a book, or get a coach to help them improve in this area.

The competencies on the right side of Figure 2 can only be learned through experience. Some of these competencies are highly differentiating, and others are considered baseline. Aspiring leaders who are lacking on one of the baseline competencies that can only be acquired through experience (the lower right quadrant), will face difficulty. Organizations recognize that these leadership qualities, like "Work Ethic," "Character," and "Empathy," are difficult to cultivate if they have not been developed earlier in life. As a result, the cost of developing them within the organization's existing leadership talent would be prohibitively high. Instead, they will tend to only select into the organization those individuals who already possess these qualities.

The competencies in the upper right corner of Figure 2 are differentiating and can only be developed through experience. These higher order competencies tend to be scarce, and the leaders who have a track record of demonstrating these capabilities will typically command respect and garner significantly higher rewards. While these characteristics are prized qualities in any leader, they are especially valuable to an organization when they have been developed within the context of that organization's specific challenges. For example, understanding the capabilities of *this organization* and the dynamics of the market that *this organization* competes in are competencies that translate directly to business strategies and results. Talented leaders brought in from the outside, even though they may have demonstrated these competencies in a different context, will need to figure out how their experience applies to this organization's specific situation.

Research on CEO succession suggests that leaders, especially more senior leaders, are not always good at applying their prior experience to a new set of organization challenges. Studies have consistently shown that CEOs hired from the outside have a lower success rate than CEOs promoted from within. Internally developed leaders deliver better results and tend to stay in their roles longer (Charan, 2005).

Back to the beginning...

This brings me back to the perplexing disconnect that launched my interest in this field nearly twenty years ago: Even though it is widely acknowledged that our most well-developed learning approaches make only a small contribution to leadership development, we have not developed a clear approach to leveraging the most valuable source of learning—on-the-job experience. If you want to learn a subject or a skill, there is a class for it. But if you want to develop yourself into a successful leader by learning from experience—the way the best leaders have done—you are on your own.

Despite the growing recognition that experience is a critical driving force in leadership development, until now we have lacked a robust, theoretically grounded framework, language, and "experience technology" to give us the control we need to leverage experience for the accelerated development of leaders.

Without such a set of tools, individuals who are trying to advance themselves as leaders have been subject to the forces of chance. While experience may be very developmental, which experiences? For whom? When? It is all too easy to find talented individuals with *years of experience* in leadership positions who feel that they have actually "had the same *one* year of experience, over and over again."

So the logical question is, "How much more successful could you be if you had the right tools to leverage your experience and help you to make the most of it?"

My hope is that you will use this book and the tools available from **FrameBreaking.com** to unlock the learning potential of your own experience and accelerate your development as a leader.

2

How Experience Accelerates Success

The contribution trajectory
of a successful leader

One of the distinguishing features of successful leadership careers is what I refer to as a steep "contribution trajectory" (Figure 3). The most successful leaders make *larger contributions* at a *faster pace* than others. Their careers are characterized by a progression of significant accomplishments in atypically rapid succession. Unsurprisingly, those making larger contributions and more significant impacts on their

Figure 3.

Illustrative comparison of differing *Contribution*
Trajectories

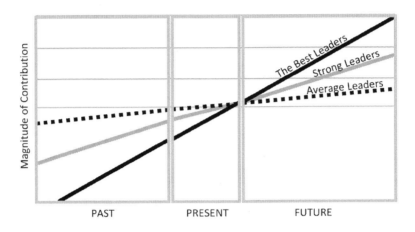

organizations tend to move up the hierarchy or become more influential. The reverse, however, does not always hold true; moving up the hierarchy is not always a good gauge of the significance of one's contributions. For that reason, the vertical axis in Figure 3 is "Magnitude of Contribution"—not, "Hierarchical Advancement."

Over the years, theorists and researchers have attempted to explain the essential reality that I depict visually in Figure 3—that some people do better than others. Is it that leaders are born with certain key leadership qualities? Or, are they "made" through a combination of determination and the circumstances in which they find themselves?

In the nineteenth and early twentieth centuries, one of the prevailing perspectives on this question became known as the "Great Man Theory" (Chemers, 2000). According to this view, leaders are simply born with more raw talent than others, and their superior talent is the cause of their success.

The opposite side of the argument puts more weight on the leader's circumstances. From this perspective, it is *opportunity or circumstance* that is the real differentiating factor; it is all about what you do with your talents, whatever they may be.

From our perspective, and with the benefit of considerable research over the past 100 years, talent and opportunity *both* play important roles in explaining a leader's success (Arvey et al. 2006; Arvey et al. 2007).

But there is more to the story. The best leaders clearly have raw talent and access to opportunities for great experiences. But a third factor that I call a *Learning Mindset* is equally important. Individuals with a Learning Mindset are curious about their work environment, their role in it, and how they are relating to others in it. Such individuals are agile learners (Lombardo and Eichinger, 2000). They constantly seek to hone a "personal theory of action" to better guide their own leadership effectiveness (Dweck, 1986; DeShon and Gillespie, 2005).

The Learning Mindset is critical to success because it is what enables a leader to get the most out of his or her experience and apply insights and learning to the pursuit of ever greater achievements. Without a Learning Mindset, the individual can easily miss the critical lessons that could have been leveraged to more effectively tackle a larger challenge in the future. In short, to make rapidly increasing contributions over time, you must be developing capabilities quickly from the experiences that you are having (sometimes *as* you're having them). And that requires a Learning Mindset.

Principle 1:
Successful leaders are shaped by the experiences they have throughout their lives

People change as a result of the experiences they have throughout their lives and careers. Whether the experiences relate to childhood lessons about values or work experiences about managing during a crisis, people glean certain lessons. The lessons learned may not be predictable (or even functional) but people have an inherent need to make sense of their life experiences:

- "What did the competition do to land that contract?"

- "Why did that employee fail?"

- "How could I have retained the star employee who quit?"

As one processes his or her experiences—thinking through the dynamics of the situations encountered to understand causality from observed events, extract lessons from experience, and use them to construct a personal "theory of action"— he or she develops a more elaborate and complex mental model for how the world works. In his book, *The Fifth Discipline*, Peter Senge refers to such theories of action as "mental models" that are "deeply ingrained assumptions, generalizations, or even pictures and images that influence how we understand the world and how we take action" (Senge, 1990, p.8).

One important factor in determining the quality of the mental model that is created is the quality of one's experiences. While it is intuitively obvious that some experiences contain more developmental potential than others, it is less clear which experiences are most critical for the development of successful leaders and what it is that leaders learn from these experiences that makes them critical.

Robust answers to these two questions would enable us to create an "experience curriculum" for leaders. Such a curriculum would specify a short list of the most developmental experiences for leaders and the lessons they teach. This list could, in turn, be used to provide those with leadership talent access to these experiences and to ensure that they learn the right lessons from them.

My own time working with clients across diverse industries suggests that this is an intuitive argument that has broad appeal. Most leadership development practitioners and aspiring leaders who express an interest in experience-based leadership development are looking for exactly such an "experience curriculum." They want an expert resource to tell them the competencies that can be learned from a specific type of experience so that the experience can be used to develop that competency. You can almost hear aspiring leaders, given a glimpse into the career experience of those who have achieved the success that they seek, saying, "give me a helping of whatever they're having."

Underlying this formulation of experience-based development is a belief that it is the *content* of the experiences that is most important. After all, the foundational research into experience-based leadership development has consistently found certain broad types of experience to be particularly important to leaders' development. Morgan McCall (2010) summarized the overarching patterns in the research as follows:

> *Study after study across organizations (e.g., Douglas, 2003; McCall & Hollenbeck, 2002a; McCall, Lombardo, & Morrison, 1988), within corporations (e.g., Valerio, 1990; Yost, Mannion-Plunkett, McKenna, & Homer, 2001; Yost & Plunkett, 2005), and in other countries (e.g., Recruit Co., Ltd., 2001) report that successful managers describe similar experiences that shaped their development. These experiences can be classi-fied roughly as early work experiences, short-term assignments, major line assignments, other people (almost always very good and very bad bosses or superiors), hardships of various kinds, and some miscellaneous events like training programs.*

The broad categories of experience McCall cites here are clearly not easy to translate into useful development experiences. However, there are plenty of other sources available that document in greater detail the experiences that tend to be associated with successful leadership careers (McCall and Hollenbeck, 2002; McCauley, Ruderman, Ohlot, and Morrow, 1994; McCall, Lombardo, and Morrisson, 1988).

Still, armed with more detailed categories of experiences, one faces the challenge of translating these generic types of experiences so that they can be practically useful for real leaders in real organizations. My colleagues and I were so intrigued by the idea of creating a useful experience curriculum for organizations that this effort became part of our consulting and research practice for nearly ten years. We worked during this decade with a number of organizations that were interested in developing an experience curriculum for their organizations. Unlike most researchers, who sought to identify a universal set of experiences that could be applied to the development of leaders in any context, we sought to identify highly specific developmental experiences valuable for the leaders within each client's organization.

We felt that a customized set of experiences would be a more practical tool for developing leaders for two reasons. First, a list of experiences specific to the challenges faced by their organization would be viewed by aspiring leaders as highly relevant to their own success—and that would motivate strong buy-in (Yost and Plunkett, 2009). Second, leaders would be able to more easily spot good development experiences if they were described in the context of their own industry and organization.

To identify the appropriate developmental experiences for leaders within each client organization, we conducted intensive interviews (two to three hours in length) with a large sample of highly successful leaders. For each interview, we used an intensive interview technique to pinpoint and explore the most developmental experiences throughout each leader's career. These interviews were all recorded and transcribed so that we could conduct content analysis and code the dynamics of each developmental experience and its associated lessons. We supplemented the interview data with senior management interviews about the strategic direction of the organization and focus groups with additional leaders from the organization.

During the course of a number of such studies we interviewed and held group discussions with over 200 highly successful leaders. The men and women we spoke with were employed in the transportation, financial services, healthcare, and publishing industries and worked in a range of roles within their organizations, including finance, IT, HR, operations, marketing, sales, and general management. The career experiences leaders shared with us were quite diverse. Some described early career experiences, such as a first supervisory experience, as particularly important to their development, while others highlighted later professional experiences, such as realigning a billion dollar business.

A shift in direction

We created an effective, though rather inefficient, method for identifying the most developmental experiences for leaders within a given organization. Conducting a large number of lengthy interviews and performing content analysis on thousands of pages of transcripts yielded great insights, but simply put, the process was quite expensive. Although the models that we created added value to our clients' leadership development efforts, we had not moved the dial as far as we had hoped.

Two vexing problems limited the value that we could deliver through customized experience models:

- It was difficult to use the most powerful developmental experiences for systematic leadership development

- The linkage between experience and learning varied from person to person

It was difficult to use the most powerful developmental experiences for systematic leadership development.

The greatest potential value from intentional experience-based development comes from helping leaders plan and learn from especially significant development experiences. The focus of my own work with clients, consistent with that of the foundational research by McCall and others, was on leaders' *most* developmental rather than on their *typical* developmental experiences.

Our research into the careers of executives in the companies for which we consulted partially replicated work done by McCall, Lombardo, and Morrison (1988) among others. Consistent with this prior research, we found that starting something from scratch, turning around a failing business, going through a leap in scope, working on an international assignment, and handling a significant failure or crisis were all highly developmental experiences. We also identified a number of context-specific developmental experiences that were unique to our client organizations, such as participating in a cross-enterprise technology-architecture project (for developing IT leaders) or re-aligning the product portfolio of an already successful business to drive organic revenue growth (for business leaders in the high tech industry).

An unintended consequence of our focus on understanding the content of highly developmental experiences was that the results were more difficult to apply broadly for leader development. The really powerful developmental experiences that we identified were often not widely available or easily leveraged for a leader's development. There are simply not enough opportunities that involve leading the start up of a new operation or going through a leap in scope to go around. Indeed, organizations *hope* not to have such an abundance of crises or failures that leaders gain extensive experience in handling them.

So the experiences we identified were useful, not as an experience curriculum, but as illustrative archetypal or idealized forms of experience. The developmental dynamics at play in the experiences we described were instructive to the extent that leaders were able to see these dynamics at work in their own work settings.

The linkage between experience and learning varies from person to person. The second problem with the content-focused approach is that, without the right tools, it is difficult to predict what a leader will learn from an experience. Steve Jobs made this important point in his now-famous commencement speech to the Stanford graduating class of 2005. When he looked back at how his experience taking a course in calligraphy influenced his later design of fonts for the Macintosh computer, he noted, "You can't connect the dots looking forward; you can only connect them looking backwards. So you have to trust that the dots will somehow connect in your future."

While it is often easy to recognize that an experience will afford "great learning opportunities," it is not as easy to delineate the specific learning opportunities it will provide and how they will benefit a given individual in the short run. I like to think of "great learning opportunities" as fertile ground for learning—whatever seed you plant in that ground is likely to grow and prosper, but the plant that sprouts will depend more upon the seed that you put in the ground than the composition of the soil. To understand the value of an experience to an individual you need to understand the interaction between the developmental opportunity and the individual. This leads to the second principle for experience-based development.

Principle 2:
Any experience can be developmental, but some experiences will be predictably more developmental for you *than others*

People are different. They often learn vastly different things from the same general type of experience. And it is not just that the experience teaches; the individual must also learn. And, what one learns from an experience will differ because of the different background and perspective that he or she brings to it and how much energy he or she devotes to understanding it.

This means that although some experiences may be fertile grounds for learning, they will not actually be useful for everyone. Just as it would make little sense to claim that a class will be "a great learning opportunity for you" without knowing your prior state of knowledge regarding the subject of the class, so too it would make little sense to claim that an experience will teach you to "delegate more effectively," without knowing something about your current delegation skills.

Furthermore, even if an experience could be developmental for a given individual, it may not provide the lessons that will help him or her achieve desired career goals. For example, a leader striving to become the head of a functional unit may not *need* another experience managing a large project within his or her area of specialty. While such an experience may provide deeper learning within a familiar area, it may not be as beneficial as developing new knowledge in unfamiliar areas. The individual may benefit more by playing a small role on a project team working on a business problem that would require him or her to develop knowledge and skills in a completely new area.

Principle 3:
Experience will only accelerate development if useful lessons are learned and applied appropriately in new situations

The first principle stated the general case that experience is critical for a leader's development. The second principle emphasized the relativity of experience—what matters is for the individual to get the *right* experience. This third principle makes the point that having the right experience is not enough to guarantee accelerated development. One must also extract the right learning, and be able to apply the newly acquired learning to new situations.

This principle can be restated as a simple formula for accelerated leadership development:

$$\text{Accelerated Development} =$$
$$(\text{Raw Talent} + \text{Experience}) \times \text{Learning Mindset} \times \text{Application}$$

This formula highlights the fact that raw talent and great experiences, while necessary, are not enough to accelerate your development. Two additional components are needed: a Learning Mindset and a focus on the intentional application of learning to new situations.

Those who actively and routinely mine their experience for insight and learning that can be integrated into or used to expand their pre-existing frameworks and knowledge get the most out of their experiences. Without such an open-minded approach, it is easy to miss important learning from even the richest developmental opportunity. Moreover, without awareness of what you are learning, you will be less able to apply what you have learned to new situations.

Missing an Opportunity or Maximizing Learning?

To illustrate the importance of bringing a Learning Mindset to one's work experience, take a moment to study Figure 4 which displays a matrix constructed from two distinct dimensions: the richness of an experience, ranging from low to high; and the Learning Mindset of the individual, ranging from low to high.

Rich experiences are "fertile ground for learning" that present individuals with significant learning opportunities. These

Figure 4.

The Learning Mindset of the individual
is a critical factor in experience-based development

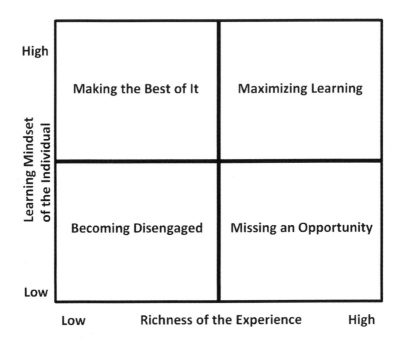

experiences often involve novel tasks and high complexity, and they require high competence to achieve acceptable performance. Experiences that are lower in richness provide fewer learning opportunities. These experiences can involve activities that are repetitive, low in complexity, and do not require a high level of competence to achieve acceptable performance.

Individuals who bring an active and intentional Learning

Mindset to experience are constantly exploring and processing. Individuals who are less consciously and intentionally focused on learning are typically more single-mindedly focused on performance and prone to leveraging just the familiar routines and habits that have worked in the past.

As depicted in Figure 4, the interaction of experience richness and Learning Mindset produces four logical outcomes: Maximizing Learning, Making the Best of It, Missing an Opportunity, and Becoming Disengaged. When organizations place a top talent person in a developmental assignment, they assume they will be Maximizing Learning. However, if the individual does not approach the situation with a Learning Mindset, he or she may well be Missing an Opportunity.

It is surprisingly difficult to consistently avoid "Missing an Opportunity." Organizations and individuals encounter the following curious Performance–Learning Paradox: *The more developmental potential an assignment provides, the less likely it is that the individual will approach it with a Learning Mindset.* This is because rich developmental experiences involve heightened performance demands, which tend to drive a "task and results" focus rather than a learning focus (DeRue and Wellman, 2009). Consider Jerry's story to see how this dynamic frequently plays out.

Example: Jerry's story

Jerry is a high potential business unit leader in the Des Moines, Iowa office of a large multinational organization. His outstanding work has caught the attention of the organization's senior leadership team. They think Jerry has the potential to take on a much larger leadership role, which would involve international respon-sibilities. In order to develop his global perspective, they decide to put him into a six-month assignment working in a branch office in Singapore. The leadership team in this office is facing a challenge in which Jerry's expertise would be a great asset.

The senior team's intent is to create a win-win situation—help solve a problem in the Singapore office and help Jerry learn how to be effective in an international context. While they have not been explicit about it, they assume that he will develop a broad range of capabilities:

- Perspective on how different markets operate

- How to work with people from a different culture

- Insight into the perspective of a cultural outsider

- Deeper appreciation of the local culture

- Relationships with key local stakeholders

When Jerry lands in Singapore, he is shuttled to a local five-star hotel, which happens to be the hotel of choice for expatriates from numerous other large corporations. The demands at the office make Jerry feel that he needs to roll up his sleeves and apply all of his expertise to help address the critical problems they are facing. So, he quickly falls into a routine of going back and forth between the hotel and the office, unwinding in the evenings by having dinner with other American expatriates that he has met at the hotel.

At the end of the assignment, everyone feels Jerry's trip was a success. Jerry is proud of having helped the Singapore office solve a significant problem, and the senior leadership team feels they made the right choice in giving Jerry the assignment.

But when the promotion opportunity comes up for Jerry, the senior team is perplexed at Jerry's utter lack of global perspective. After the CEO meets with Jerry, he tells the rest of the team, "It's like Jerry has never been out of Iowa. I don't think he learned anything in Singapore!"

Jerry's story is a clear example of Missing an Opportunity. Jerry did not bring a Learning Mindset to what had the potential to be a very rich experience. Instead, he focused solely on achieving success on the task.

Questions about Jerry's story

1) What could Jerry have done differently to learn more from his experience at the Singapore office?

2) What could the Senior Leadership team have done differently to ensure Jerry learned what they wanted him to learn?

3) Who is most responsible for the poor learning outcome in this scenario? Why?

4) Do you tend to approach new work challenges with a single-minded performance focus? What could you do to make sure that you don't miss learning opportunities?

A different perspective

While in retrospect it may be easy to see the developmental potential of an experience such as Jerry's international assignment, it is surprisingly easy to find ourselves falling into familiar patterns and missing the learning. So, when we face less obviously developmental territory, it is even more important to adopt a Learning Mindset. For example, had Jerry taken an assignment in Omaha, the opportunities for learning would have been much subtler. Without a Learning Mindset, the talented individual who seeks bigger challenges and more visible contributions is at risk for finding the comparatively less attractive assignment in Omaha as an opportunity for stagnation rather than growth. Hence, the risks of Becoming Disengaged or exiting the situation are high.

Early career professionals are often concerned about getting access to impressive-sounding opportunities. As such, they are focused on what will "look good on a resume." What is often missed is that the mindset the individual brings to an opportunity is almost as important as the "quality" of the opportunity itself.

With a Learning Mindset, one can find opportunities for Making the Best of It and learning from even mundane experiences. One executive I spoke with described the critical learning he got from working in a men's clothing store early in his career:

> *I worked for a manager who was obsessed with quality. One of his pet projects was keeping the sock display neat and tidy. It seems like a small thing, but I learned that it is attention to quality in the small things that adds up to create a great customer experience. Now, whenever I see frayed edges in our customer experience, I think about the sock display...*

The lesson here is that if you approach your experiences with a Learning Mindset, you can learn from even the most mundane experiences.

To learn from experience, you need to *experience the learning*

The introduction to the first principle in this chapter noted that we have a tendency to actively make sense of the world we live in. Although sense-making is a natural part of being human, we also have a powerful countervailing tendency to stop seeking meaning once we have developed a sufficiently robust working theory to explain our experience.

To conserve our mental energy in the face of the otherwise overwhelming sensory complexity of the world, we limit our attention and employ shortcuts, both in our perceptions and our thinking about the world. Novelty and unfamiliarity trigger us to seek an explanation for things, signaling that there is something for us to learn. Once we have constructed a reasonable working theory to explain that which was previously unexplained, we file this new knowledge away and shift our attention elsewhere. And we don't revisit it.

Unless, that is, we face some new reality that conflicts so directly with the mental model we have constructed that we are forced to face the fact that our view of the world is flawed or incomplete.

These competing tendencies—to learn and expand our mental models of the world based on our experiences and to act using mental models based on shortcuts—make it difficult to bring a Learning Mindset to everything that we do.

Psychologists studying human perception and cognition have documented how a wide range of perceptual and cognitive shortcuts lead us to predictably flawed mental models. Noting just a few of the insights from research on perception and cognition—Selective Perception, the Fundamental Attribution Error, Self-Serving Bias, and Halo Effects—should serve to make the point that we can all be better students of our own experience.

Selective Perception. Because the brain can only process a small amount of the stimuli it receives from the senses, it naturally limits the information it attends to by prioritizing some information and placing it into the foreground of our mind, while relegating everything else to the background (Cooper and Argyris, 1998). Aside from basic perceptual information needed to navigate our world, the brain will tend to foreground information that "catches our interest."

If you consider buying a new car, for example, it will suddenly seem that there are lots of people driving around in the make and model car that you are considering purchasing. This is not due to a sudden surge in sales of the car. Rather, you start to notice the cars that have always been there because now you have been thinking about them.

The Fundamental Attribution Error. When we observe the actions of others, we naturally make assumptions—or attributions—about why they are doing what they are doing (Cooper and Argyris, 1998). The driver who cuts you off on the freeway is doing so because "he is an idiot!" The co-worker who shows up at the office late is viewed as "not committed" or, perhaps, "lazy."

These examples highlight our deep-seated tendency to attribute the behavior of others to internal, stable qualities of the other person rather than to external factors. We don't pause to speculate about various explanations for the driver's behavior: "Perhaps he didn't see us," "Perhaps he was avoiding a road hazard," or "Perhaps he was pre-occupied because he just learned of a family crisis."

While you may quickly dismiss these explanations as far-reaching (and you would be right), the driver's behavior provides just as much evidence for any one of these external causes as it does that he or she possesses a character flaw. Yet, research on the fundamental attribution error consistently shows that we routinely make internal attributions like these without a second thought.

Self-Serving Bias. While we tend to blame the failures and shortcomings of others on their personal capabilities, we tend to diminish our *own* role in failures and shift the blame to external factors (Frasier et al. 2004). For example, in failing to perform on an assignment, there is a natural tendency to blame external factors, "I didn't get clear instructions; the target kept moving; there weren't enough resources available, etc."

In addition, we have an equally strong tendency to overemphasize our own role in successes rather than attributing success to external factors out of our control. So, in the face of a successful project, it is not uncommon to attribute the success to things that you did, such as "I rallied the team to success," "I delivered a persuasive pitch," or, "I worked hard and that made the difference." These may be partially or entirely valid reasons for success—or they might be self-serving rationalizations!

Halo Effects. When seeking information, we tend to be unduly influenced by one or a few characteristics that stand out prominently (Cooper and Argyris, 1998). For example, when hiring an employee, if the applicant attended the same school as the interviewer, it can lead to generally positive view of the candidate—even if there are other qualities that are more important to the individual's potential for success in the organization. The tendency to develop generally positive impressions from a single positive characteristic is referred to as a *positive halo*, while developing generally negative impressions from a single negative characteristic is referred to as a *negative halo*.

These limitations, and many others, have the combined effect of constraining the quality of our mental models of the world. How can you routinely draw the right lessons from experience given that these thinking shortcuts mean that you:

- Miss critical details (selective perception),

- Attribute the wrong motives to other people's behaviors (fundamental attribution error),

- Overstate or understate your own impact on the success or failure of the effort (self-serving bias), and

- Unduly influence the assessment of a person or situation because of one feature that stands out in your mind (halo effects)?

Regardless of the quality of our thought processes regarding a situation, we will draw certain conclusions or form impressions and opinions. More self-aware and deliberate consideration is likely to yield better outcomes, but also takes more energy. This is why it is critical that you make conscious decisions to focus your attention and energy on the right things.

Learning and the Invisible Gorilla

If you are one of the millions of viewers who have participated in the experiment on Attentional Blindness by Chrisopher Chabris and Daniel Simons, you probably already have a deep appreciation for how easy it is to miss key details in an experience because you are focused on the wrong things. There is a clear parallel between Attentional Blindness and a kind of blindness to learning.

In Chabris and Simons's experiment, which aired during prime time on a national news program, viewers are asked to count the number of times that a group of basketball players wearing white shirts (while others wear dark shirts), pass a basketball back and forth during a short video clip. (SPOILER ALERT! If you have not participated in the experiment, and would like to do so, I suggest that you stop reading here. The next paragraph will spoil the experiment for you. You can experience the experiment by watching the short video titled "Attentional Blindness" that can be accessed from the FrameBreaking.com website).

To count the number of passes requires that you direct your attention single-mindedly on the players wearing white shirts and the ball, and block out the chaotic motion of the other basketball players. The net result is that a majority of participants in the study fail to notice the fact that, part way through the video clip, a person in a gorilla suit walks into the center of the screen, beats his chest, and exits the screen. *More than half of those who participate in the experiment fail to see the person in the gorilla suit, even though he stands in the middle of the screen!* In fact, Chabris and Simons (2010) titled their book detailing this Attentional Blindness phenomenon, *The Invisible Gorilla*.

I liken the learning in our work experiences to the invisible gorilla. It is easy to focus so intently on the "performance ball," that you miss the learning opportunities right in front of you. We miss the learning because we are devoting so much precious mental energy to our job performance. And, when we are successful at what we are doing, we are not likely to stop and explore the reasons why we are successful. Instead, we are much more likely to attribute our success to our personal capabilities, e.g., "I'm a great communicator" or "I'm a team player." Such self-serving attributions lead one to conclude that there is nothing more to be learned. When this happens, we have slipped into the perspective that, "If it ain't broke, don't fix it!"

But, if you don't reflect on *why* you are successful, you may be getting by on strengths while not recognizing significant development needs or even potential "fatal flaws." External factors may have played a larger role in your success than you are acknowledging, and, not realizing this, you miss an opportunity to learn. For example, the product manager who starts to see a positive sales trend in a historically tough product category may have a natural tendency to see that improvement as a result of his or her own actions. This will lead to attributions such as, "my advertising campaign is working," or, "the new organization structure I put in place is effective." The true causes for the improvement, however, may be other factors such as a change in consumer demand driven by external factors. For extreme case examples where a macro trend has had a significant impact on the performance of a product or product category, think— "health benefits of whole grains" and "whole grain cereal"; "worst recession since the great depression" and "low-price consumer goods"; or "fear of bird flu pandemic" and "hand sanitizer." Failing to reflect on the true causes of success, the manager may develop significantly flawed mental models for success. Unfortunately, it is not uncommon to recognize these needs too late, only in the face of a significant failure.

Because we are most familiar with making sense of our experiences when we fail, most people think failing is the biggest source of learning. This isn't necessarily the case. People do learn a lot from failure, but that is mostly because people tend not to actively seek insight and meaning from their successes. Instead, they simply celebrate (or even take for granted) having achieved desired results.

If you can't get over it, go around it...

In order to learn from experience, you have to be open to *experiencing the learning*. But, given the built-in limitations of human perception and cognition, is this something that you can get better at?

Think for a moment of a woman who needs to manage a large number of tasks in order to be successful. From time to time, important deadlines are missed because she simply cannot remember everything she needs to do. It is too mentally taxing to keep in mind all of the information about the various tasks—key dates, steps, responsibilities, etc. This person could approach the task of improving performance by attempting to expand her memory to ensure that nothing is forgotten. There are various mnemonic devices that can be learned, but expanding memory will likely take a lot of hard work. And, despite using the best tools and approaches available, her desired results might not be achieved.

But there is another, easier approach—she can use a task list. If the individual invests even a small amount of energy into using an appropriate tool, the tool can overcome the cognitive limitation.

This basic principle is the approach that I have followed in this book. Instead of trying to improve your ability to think abstractly about experience and learning, I have created tools to assist you with several key thought processes:

- What have I learned from my past experiences?

- How can I learn more from what I am doing today?

- How can I choose development opportunities that will help me to achieve my career goals?

The FrameBreaking model and the tools available from **FrameBreaking.com** will give you a new way to look at all of your experiences and what you can learn from them.

3

The FrameBreaking Model—
A Tool to Leverage Your Experience

Frame (of Reference): The context, viewpoint, or set of evaluative criteria within which a person's perception and thinking generally occur, and which constrains their judgments, decisions, and actions.

- Adapted from the Dictionary of Modern Thought (Bullock, 1999)

Most people are familiar with the term "frame of reference." While we are not typically aware of the "frames" that we carry with us, they shape our view of the world in a very fundamental way. We generally only become aware of our frames when our assumptions are violated. As long as our frames are functional, we use them to guide our actions.

I use the term "FrameBreaking" to describe a particular type of experience that forces one to significantly shift his or her thinking. In these experiences, people find themselves encountering situations which defy their existing frames and require them to rethink their assumptions and develop new frames of reference to guide their action or face failure (McCall, 1998).

To illustrate the FrameBreaking concept, think for a moment of a leader who goes through a sudden leap in the scope of her responsibilities—from having responsibility for a small staff of three people, to having responsibility for 60, including a large group from another department. If the leader were to attempt to leverage the techniques she learned with her small staff to lead an organization 20 times larger, she would fail. With a small staff, she was able to leverage her own task expertise and step in to bail out her people if they got in over their heads. If she attempted to use that approach with a larger group, she would quickly become overwhelmed. She must rethink how to lead in order to be successful... she must "break her frame" for effective leadership and develop a new perspective.

There is an intentionally destructive connotation to the term FrameBreaking. When things break, it is not always easy, or even possible, to fix them. While it will become clear that these experiences can be highly developmental, they can also be highly risky for the individual and the organization. The individual might fail, and if the leader holds a senior position, there may be substantial organizational risk. This is why organizations tend to be reluctant to place people in these experiences.

While the FrameBreaking Model is named after the FrameBreaking experience because it is the most developmental type of experience, the model describes three additional types of experience: Delivering, Mastering, and Broadening. And, as will be discussed, the four experiences all play an important role in one's development and career success.

Finally, I use the phrase "FrameBreaking Leadership Development" to refer to a shift in perspective about how to develop leaders, from formal classroom or other forms of mediated learning to an intentional approach for on-the-job, experience-based development.

A new way to think about experience

The FrameBreaking Leadership Development Model provides a unique lens for *any individual* to identify the developmental potential of *any experience*.

Two fundamental dimensions are combined to create the FrameBreaking model: Intensity and Stretch. These dimensions are conceptually distinct measures of the developmental potential of an experience. Each dimension is defined in the sections that follow, and then they are combined to present the full model.

Intensity—"Handling *More* Performance Demands"

Intensity measures the relative degree or magnitude of certain key dynamics present in a work situation. For example:

- Are there tight deadlines? (Time Pressure)

- Are you the one in charge of the situation? (Holistic responsibility)

- Is there a lot at stake? (Risk)

These and the other sub-dimensions of Intensity are listed in Figure 5. Experiences that involve high levels of these sub-dimensions have the potential to be developmental because they present particularly high performance demands. When you are doing work that pushes you to perform at a higher level, you need to be fully engaged and learn new things under pressure. You can't rely on doing things the way you have done them in the past or "go through the motions" and be successful. You need to thrive in order to survive, hence the acronym THRIVE in Figure 5.

One General Manager from a financial services firm described the high Intensity he experienced leading his team through crisis in the aftermath of 9/11:

> *Our business was half way up the tower in One World Trade Center. When the towers collapsed, everything was thrown into chaos. We all got out, and after a few days, when the dust had started to settle, we got together—all 110 of us—in a hotel conference room a couple of blocks from Ground Zero and started to regroup. That first day, it was*

Figure 5.

Defining Intensity—THRIVE

Time pressure
Requiring action within specific, aggressive time constraints and with high costs for delays, versus being open-ended with no time constraints

Holistic responsibility
Involving responsibility for an entire outcome or set of outcomes, versus participation as one of many contributors to an outcome

Risk
Involving high financial, reputational, or other stakes and a moderate risk of failure, versus low stakes and low risk of failure

Impact
Involving results that are critical for business survival, profit, growth, or other success metric, versus being a discretionary activity which yields nice-to-have results

Visibility
Involving visibility at the highest levels and to a large population, versus being private or visible to only a small, local population

Expectations
Degree to which others expect success versus have no or low expectations for results.

all just about sharing our stories, working through some of the personal trauma, and letting everyone know that we were all in this together.

Pretty quickly we had to turn our attention to the business crisis we were facing. We didn't have all the disaster recovery plans in place that we should have—we were a small group—and if we couldn't get our operations back up in two weeks, we would be out of business.

When I laid out the stark reality, someone shouted out, "We're not going to let some $@#!'ing terrorist take this company from us!" And that was a turning point. We all just dug in and did whatever we needed to do.

I learned a lot about managing in a crisis that I had never been taught. I saw people operating under incredible pressure, and I developed an awareness of the amazing things that people are capable of achieving. When people need to rise to the challenge, they will. I have kept that insight with me every day since then, and I expect the most from people.

While a situation high in Intensity will require you to handle more Time pressure, Risk, Visibility, etc., it will not necessarily push you to learn things from an area beyond your prior expertise, preparation, or experience. To be successful, you may need to dig down deep to achieve results that you didn't think you were capable of achieving. But that need not involve doing different kinds of work or interacting with different kinds of people.

Work situations that push you to learn different things, outside your area of expertise or prior experience are described by the second dimension: Stretch.

Stretch—"Handling *different* performance demands"

Stretch describes the extent to which an experience pushes you outside your area of expertise, background, or preparation. For example, if you were to ask an IT manager to participate in a sales call that might be routine for a sales professional, the IT manager would likely feel pushed outside his or her "comfort zone." How do I act on a sales call? What does the customer want to know? What do I need to know about what we are selling? These and other questions would likely be raised because the manager's frame of reference lacks information applicable to the new situation.

Figure 6 outlines the dimensions, described with the acronym REACH, that combine to describe the extent of Stretch that a person encounters in a situation.

While Stretch describes situations in which a person needs to operate differently, it is conceptually independent of a situation's Intensity. For example, if an IT manager were asked to participate in a large cross-functional task force to develop a new approach to employee communications, he or she would probably have little prior experience to draw on. So, the experience would involve some degree of Stretch. However, as merely a participant on the task force, with little or no formal responsibility, the level of Intensity would probably be relatively low.

International assignments, too, can provide a high level of Stretch, without necessarily involving a high level of Intensity. One of the financial services executives from the United Kingdom that I spoke with described what she learned about communication from an assignment in the United States:

Figure 6
Defining Stretch—REACH

Relationships
Involving the need to interact with people who hold differing perspectives, outlooks, or viewpoints

Expertise or knowledge
Involving the need to develop expertise or knowledge in an unfamiliar area in order to be successful

Adaptability
Involving the need to handle more ambiguity than one is used to

Context
Involving the need to work within a different function/department/area or culture

How-to skills
Involving the need to spend time doing things he or she doesn't know how to do

I made the move from London to the States, and I think I was here for about two months before I realized that, although I was hearing what people were saying, I wasn't understanding it. And, what's more, they weren't understanding me. I was literally talking past my direct reports, and I didn't realize it. And, that really taught me to listen and to question and to have people feed back to me what they heard. You think, "We all speak the same language, so communication should be easy," but actually if we spoke a different language it would be easier because I'd know if you were speaking French to me or Arabic or whatever it is.

I remember a team meeting where I suddenly realized we were not on the same wavelength. I thought I had been very clear about what needed to get done. And then the team had come back with project plans and initiatives that were completely wide of the mark. I realized in that moment that we were just not using language in a way that allowed for clear communication.

That really, really taught me both about listening and confirming understanding. It made me passionate about clear specifications. Now I really focus on "Well, what are the real requirements? What do I really have to get done here? Do we all understand what we need to get done?"

Are you Leveraging or Learning?

When evaluating an experience using the THRIVE and REACH dimensions, a key question is, "Am I leveraging capabilities that I have already developed, or am I learning new capabilities?" To illustrate this point, consider the example of a manager who goes from managing a one million dollar budget to managing a twenty million dollar budget. Clearly, the larger budget involves a higher level of risk, and that will mean the manager needs to handle this responsibility with greater skill and discipline. This experience will likely present the manager with an opportunity for learning. If the numbers were reversed, however, and the manager went from managing a twenty million dollar budget to a one million dollar budget, the manager would be able to leverage skills learned from managing the larger budget to more effectively manage the smaller budget.

Situations that push you to handle greater overall levels of Intensity and Stretch can be thought of as opportunities to *learn* new capabilities. Situations that present you with an overall level of Intensity and Stretch that you have already handled competently can be thought of as opportunities to *leverage* your capabilities.

FrameBreaking Leadership Development:
A subjective, dynamic, descriptive, and developmental model of experience

If we combine the Intensity and Stretch dimensions together, we create a model (shown in Figure 7) for looking at experiences, careers, and personal development. The four quadrants of the model describe four broad but distinct types of experiences: Delivering, Mastering, Broadening, and FrameBreaking.

Figure 7.
The FrameBreaking Model

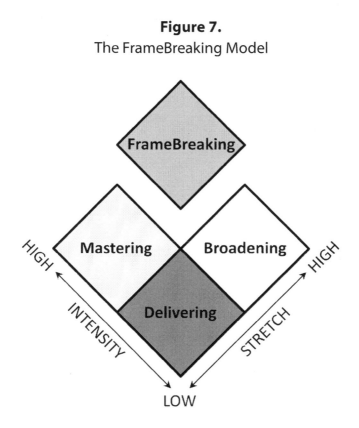

The model should be viewed as subjective, dynamic, descriptive, and developmental. Each of these qualities of the model is addressed in the following sections.

Subjective: *Intensity and Stretch as experienced by the individual*

Intensity and Stretch are not objective properties of a developmental opportunity, but properties of the interaction between the opportunity and the individual. Figures 5 and 6 describe an illustrative range of values for each sub-dimension of Intensity and Stretch. However, the important factor for understanding the developmental potential of an experience for an individual is the individual's *subjective experience* of Intensity and Stretch.

To illustrate the point, imagine that you identify a group of people within a large retail organization who have all indicated on a survey that their most developmental career experience involved what they describe as "managing a turnaround." You decide to talk to three of them—the CEO, the head of HR, and a store manager.

The CEO. When the CEO describes her most developmental experience, she talks about the turnaround of a failing five hundred million dollar business unit. As you listen to her gripping story, it becomes clear why the experience stands out to her: referring to Figures 5 and 6, she describes the situation as involving a higher level of Intensity and Stretch than she had previously experienced in her career.

The head of HR. The next individual that you speak with is the head of the human resources function for the same multi-billion dollar business. His turnaround story involves inheriting an HR group in disarray and lacking credibility. His story has some of the same turnaround elements as the CEO's, but the stakes are not as objectively high (his budget is only fifty million dollars, the number of affected employees is smaller, etc.). Yet, the story is equally gripping, and it is clear that he experienced the turnaround of the department as involving higher levels of Intensity and Stretch than he had previously experienced in his career.

The store manager. Finally, you speak with the manager of one of the company's retail outlets. His turnaround story involves turning around a failing store, which had fallen into disrepair, had customer service and employee problems, and was losing $50,000 per year. Though the stakes are objectively much smaller than in either of the other two stories, this individual describes his experience as involving higher levels of Intensity and Stretch than he had previously experienced in his career.

These examples use a single type of experience, a turnaround, to illustrate that the extent of Intensity and Stretch in an experience reflects the subjective experience of the individual. The fifty thousand dollar stakes for the manager, and the multi-million dollar stakes for both the CEO and the head of human resources were experienced by each as high in Intensity and Stretch

Dynamic: *You move through the different types of experiences throughout your career*

The model is dynamic, and throughout a career most people will spend time in each of the four types of experience. A typical career will involve a wide range of experiences from those that push the individual to develop in new ways, to those that involve utilizing well-established skills on familiar ground. Moreover, any given assignment may involve a mix of the familiar and the new.

Each experience type offers different value to individuals at different points in their careers. Spending a great deal of time in just one quadrant, however, and less time in the other quadrants can have implications for how one develops. For example, spending large amounts of time in the Mastering quadrant tends to lead one to develop highly specialized skills and experience. Musicians, athletes, and chess masters are a few examples of pure experts who are at home in Mastering experiences. They seek opportunities to push themselves within their chosen fields to higher and higher levels of attainment.

The FrameBreaking model can help you to reflect on patterns in how you have been developing throughout your career, and what the implications of those patterns may be for your ability to achieve your career goals. Have you spent concentrated time in some areas and neglected others? If so, has that pattern been the result of an intentional choice, or is it a pattern that you can seek to change?

Descriptive: *No one experience type is better than the others*

Although the model is referred to as the FrameBreaking model, that is not intended to suggest that FrameBreaking is a "better" type of experience for leader development. These experiences offer the greatest developmental potential, but they also present the greatest risk for failure. And, it may not be necessary for an aspiring leader to take such risks in order to achieve desired career goals.

Developmental: *Reflects growth of capabilities over time*

Think of the size of the Delivering quadrant as your level of capability. Early in your career, your Delivering quadrant is relatively small. You have not acquired a very large or broad repertoire of experiences and are not able to make large contributions to an organization. Early on, many work activities are experienced as either Mastering, Broadening, or even FrameBreaking, because they are outside of your small, but growing, Delivering zone.

Over time, as you engage in various Mastering, Broadening and FrameBreaking experiences, the size of your Delivering zone grows, and your capacity to contribute increases.

The developmental nature of the model is shown in the progressive growth of an individual's capabilities in Figure 8. The top half the figure represents a junior sales person who has not yet developed basic sales skills. For this individual, conducting a sales call on his or her own would involve a high level of Intensity (lower levels of Intensity would be associated with observing another person making a sales call or assisting in the sales call, but not having responsibility to lead the effort). As basic sales skills are mastered, the individual's capabilities grow and might be represented by the bottom half of Figure 8. Here, conducting a sales call has become routine, and now the higher level of Intensity might come from training others or leading a sales team. The important point to note is that, as your capabilities grow, your Delivering zone grows. This means that work that was once experienced as high in Intensity or Stretch becomes routine.

Figure 8.
Intensity and Stretch dimensions are dynamic, and change over time as one's capabilities grow

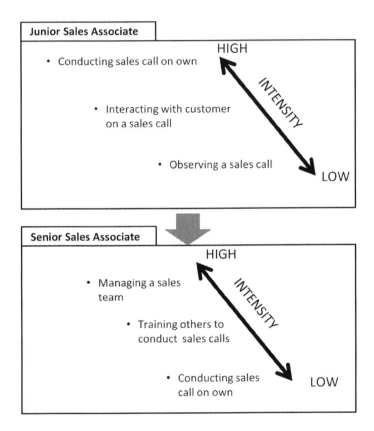

A point of clarification about "Stretch assignments"

Many organizations use the term "Stretch assignment" to describe a "great development opportunity." But this term tends to be used rather loosely. It commonly refers to any situation that combines powerful developmental dynamics, such as "high level of challenge," "handling large stakes," "using new skills," or "operating in a different context." While all of these dimensions may be useful for development, they engage the individual in different ways and drive different learning outcomes.

The FrameBreaking Model separates developmental dynamics into the two distinct dimensions of Intensity and Stretch to provide a more useful language for thinking about the features of an experience that make it more or less developmental for a given individual. With the sub-dimensions of THRIVE and REACH outlined in Figures 5 and 6, the model provides eleven dimensions for developing rich assessments of the developmental dynamics of an experience for an individual. These dimensions are incorporated into easy-to-use online tools available at **FrameBreaking.com** for those interested in applying the FrameBreaking Model.

The chapters that follow explore each of the four types of experience in greater detail to assist you with applying the model to your own career.

4

Delivering

The assignment was a perfect fit for me. At my former employer, I had been asked to do the same kind of work, and I loved it. This was a great opportunity to work with customers, which I love doing, and to meet a target that I was pretty sure I could meet. It was a real confidence builder, because I was looked to as an expert in this stuff, and I enjoyed being in that kind of role.

– Director, financial services company

Delivering

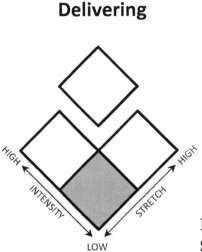

Intensity: Low - Moderate
Stretch: Low - Moderate

Individual sees as: *"Doing my job"*

- Applying well-developed skills

- Leveraging strengths

- Developing a sense of accomplishment

- Building confidence in abilities

Organization sees as: *"Best person-job fit"*

- Predictable performance

- Low risk of failure

- Maximum short-term results

- Typical approach: Hold employees in place, because they are most productive in the short-term

Delivering

In a Delivering experience, you deal with situations that involve levels of Stretch and Intensity that you have handled before. When you are in the Delivering zone, you are in a performance sweet spot, doing work that uses your skills and positions you to be an effective contributor to the organization.

Because Delivering experiences do not involve encountering higher levels of Intensity or Stretch, they tend not to offer as much obvious developmental potential as the other types of experience; you are already fully qualified and capable of delivering results on work within your Delivering zone. In this respect, Delivering is more about *exercising* competence than *developing* competence.

Even so, Delivering experiences are attractive to individuals and to the organizations in which they work. They build confidence and provide the individual with the opportunity to use their proven skills and achieve results valued by the organization. When an organization needs to recruit and hire for a job opening, it marshals whatever forces it can to place people into Delivering experiences. This is referred to as ensuring a "Person-Job fit." Achieving a good fit is a means of reducing risk for the organization. So, putting people into Delivering experiences is generally viewed as a win-win situation.

It is important to distinguish between the need to spend time in the Delivering zone and seeking to use a Delivering experience for your development. We all need to spend time in the Delivering zone in order to succeed at work. Reliably delivering results is a basic expectation and requirement for keeping your job. Moreover, proving yourself through a series of Delivering experiences—"paying your dues"—is often a prerequisite to getting access to larger, more developmental opportunities.

Learning by Delivering

While Delivering experiences do not pack the same *obvious* developmental punch as the other types of experience, they play an important role in your progress toward career goals. Delivering experiences can help you:

- Deepen your perspective within a familiar area

- Build your track record of accomplishments

- Leverage your skills, knowledge and expertise

Deepen your perspective within a familiar area

Time spent in the Delivering zone does not significantly build your capacity for handling bigger or different challenges, but it can provide valuable opportunities to *see more variety* of challenges and to *see things over time*.

Seeing more variety. Experts, such as consultants, are very comfortable in the Delivering zone. They spend a considerable amount of time honing expertise within an area of specialization through Mastering experiences to create a solid and marketable set of skills and knowledge. Once they have developed that expertise, they seek opportunities to apply it. Each engagement for the experienced consultant represents a Delivering experience (no client would hire a consultant if they thought otherwise).

Delivering

Even though a consultant spends much of his or her time in the Delivering zone, he or she can still learn. Being exposed to a wide variety of problems, even when they are all within the Delivering zone, deepens your understanding of the dynamics at work within your area of expertise. For example, I worked as a talent management and leadership development consultant for a number of years. One of the core skills I developed early on was competency modeling—identifying the competencies (e.g., Strategic Thinking, Influence and Persuasion, etc.) that differentiate the best performers from others within a given client organization. In my first year as a full-time consultant, I was involved in the development of seven competency models for large organizations. By the time I completed work on the seventh model, I was proficient in model development. Developing another model would be a Delivering experience.

When I moved on to another consulting firm and worked in competency modeling, I was leveraging my competency modeling knowledge. But that did not mean that I stopped learning. I began to develop higher-order insights—how different organizations view competencies, the importance of stakeholder involvement, and what models look like in different environments (e.g., retail, technology, or publishing). I was operating squarely in my Delivering zone, but still gaining valuable insight.

Encountering a wider variety of challenges and situations, even those that you clearly have the ability to handle, builds a key capability for leaders: pattern recognition. Pattern recognition is critical because it shapes your judgment. Having a broad array of experiences within your area of expertise gives you richer mental models to leverage in future situations.

Seeing things over time. Spending time in the Delivering zone can also be valuable because it gives you insight into dynamics that play out over time. Consultants gain unique perspective because they are in a position to work in many diverse situations. They are called in at specific points by organizations that seek to leverage the consultant's expertise—they are needed to do the market research, develop the strategic plan, create the competency model, etc. But consultants do not usually have the chance to see how their work is implemented and the impact that it has on an organization.

I have experienced this in my own career. After being a consultant, I took a position heading the executive development function for a large corporation. One of my first tasks was to introduce a competency model for the top 500 leaders. While I had developed many competency models as a consultant, this was a learning experience because this time I was on the *inside* of the organization. This gave me the chance to see how a definition of leadership becomes part of the company culture. After a year or two, I heard people talking about leaders using the language of the model as a natural part of their conversation. Seeing the process of competency model implementation from this insider perspective gave me new insight that I could not have appreciated without seeing it unfold over time.

If top talent leaders move too quickly out of the Delivering zone, they risk developing a skill set that looks more like that of a consultant than that of an executive. The plans the consultant delivers may look great on paper, but they don't necessarily work. Similarly, leaders may seek to implement plans that look good on paper and move on before they get the chance to learn that they don't (or didn't) work. Without staying in place long enough to experience the long-term impact of your actions, you may be doomed to continually repeat mistakes that you don't even know you are making. One CEO I spoke with cited his experience at a large, fast-paced beverage company:

> *We realized that you need to keep people in place long enough to see that they weren't really getting the great results that they thought they were... they needed to learn that some of the stuff they put in place didn't really work...*

Some organizations describe the need for a leader to spend enough time in a certain situation as needing some "seasoning" or needing to spend more "time in role."

Building your track record of accomplishments

Working in an area in which you have proven skills provides an opportunity to excel and make important contributions to the organization. Because the challenges you face in a Delivering experience are generally familiar to you, you have a good chance of excelling. That is not to suggest that Delivering experiences are without challenge—even though Delivering experiences involve working in a familiar area, they can still contain high levels of certain dimensions of Intensity and Stretch (e.g., Time Pressure, Risk, Expertise, etc.).

If you are able to deliver great results consistently, you may gain access to others (possibly higher-level executives) with whom you would not normally interact. Still, you need to balance the extent to which achieving key results will be a source of power and influence with the possibility that delivering the same results repeatedly may not prepare you to take on larger responsibilities and make larger contributions. It would be nice if the saying "good work will eventually be rewarded" were always true. Anyone who has worked in large organizations for any length of time has to acknowledge, though, that things do not always work that way.

Leveraging your skills, knowledge, and expertise

Delivering experiences play to your strengths and give you the chance to use valued skills. Most doctors, lawyers, musicians, airline pilots, accountants, et al. simply seek the opportunity to practice the skills they have already developed. In a similar fashion, accomplished leaders can gain a sense of satisfaction and increased self-efficacy from the normal work of leadership—assessing strategic options, articulating a vision, solving complex problems, and dealing with any variety of problems that they have previously faced in one shape or another.

The Delivering Trap

Staying in the Delivering zone can be appealing. Once you have mastered a task and are able to deliver results with reduced effort, it is easy to fall into a comfort zone (Figure 9). If you spend too much time in the Delivering quadrant, you miss the opportunity to develop new skills, expand your

Figure 9.

Delivering Trap *– Not balancing the need for challenge with the opportunity to get results while in the comfort zone*

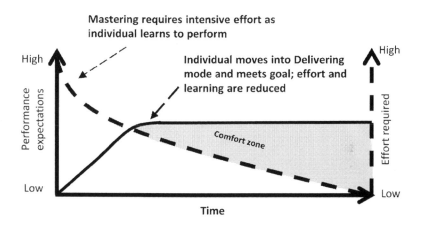

perspective, and learn what you need to make a larger contribution to the organization. Unfortunately, this may eventually lead to de-motivation and disengagement.

If you think that you may have slipped into this Delivering Trap, reflect on this question: "Am I having the same year of experience for the second, third, or fourth year in a row?"

If the answer to this question is "yes," it may mean that you are in the Delivering Trap. Rather than learning and expanding your mental models of the world, you are staying in familiar territory and leveraging what you have done in the past. This may be sufficient to enjoy continued success in your current role, but it is unlikely to enable you to "change the game" and succeed on a larger playing field.

Should I consider a Delivering experience?

The following questions can help you decide whether a Delivering experience would help you to achieve your career goals.

1) How would a Delivering experience help me make progress toward my career goal?

   - Do I need to build my track record or "pay my dues"?

   - Would additional experience in a familiar area significantly enhance my chances of future success? How?

   - What gaps in my experience would be filled by a Delivering experience? Are these "must-have" experiences that I will need to achieve my career goal?

2) Would Delivering provide me the opportunity to make a significant contribution to the organization?

   If solving a key problem or getting important results is within your Delivering zone, it can lead to increased visibility and added opportunity to learn from senior leaders.

   - If I achieve the results associated with Delivering, will it make a significant contribution to the organization? What three things could I do to meet or exceed expectations?

3) What is the opportunity cost?

   Remember that pursuing a Delivering experience would mean not engaging in some other, different development experience.

   •   Would working in a familiar area and delivering results be the best way to make progress toward my career goal at this time?

4) Am I passionate about the work I would do in a Delivering experience?

   •   Do I want to continue working in the area in which I have already established myself with similar tasks, similar issues, and similar types of people?

   •   When I think about what it would *feel like* to do the work I would be doing in a Delivering experience, am I motivated and energized?

5) Have I had enough Delivering?

   If you repeatedly have similar types of Delivering experiences, you may find yourself getting de-motivated and disengaged.

   •   Would I learn enough from a Delivering experience to feel that I am continuing to grow and develop?

5

Broadening

This job involved getting out of my comfort zone in more ways than one. It was an offsite assignment. I flew down to Nashville every Monday and flew back every Friday. Nashville felt as far away from Chicago as did Pluto. People looked at your eyes when you were in the elevator and wanted to strike up a conversation with you. It was just a totally different world. I mean, there was just a different set of relationship expectations than you have at work here. Your people and your peers are more like family than they are in a work environment elsewhere.

– General Manager, large publishing company

Broadening

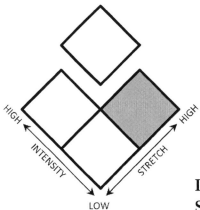

Intensity: Low - Moderate
Stretch: Moderate - High

Individual sees as: *"Developing perspective, expanding skills"*

* Developing new and different skills

* Learning outside area of expertise

* Expanding knowledge and experience

Organization sees as: *"Preparing leaders for the future"*

* Long-term investment in future talent

* Uncertain payoff

* Typical approach: Use these experiences with early career high potentials to broaden their management skills (e.g., job rotation programs)

In a Broadening experience, you deal with situations that involve a higher level of Stretch than you are accustomed to, but with only a low to moderate level of Intensity. Although most developmental experiences involve some degree of Intensity, the learning thrust in a Broadening experience is primarily related to the Stretch of the experience. That Stretch stems from the need to face different types of situations—challenges, people, and contexts. The defining feature of a Broadening experience is that you need to relate to others, think, or act in different and unfamiliar ways.

Because Broadening experiences involve acquiring knowledge and skills or developing perspectives you don't already possess, these experiences provide a chance to think differently and develop different capabilities.

In my work with IT leaders, I found that some of the most developmental experiences involved simply being a member of a cross-functional team evaluating business processes to improve technology systems. Even those who were in a passive role on such teams found the project valuable because they were learning things about the business they would not have had any other opportunity to learn—how information needs to flow across the company in order to meet business needs and how that information is used by each business function.

Broadening experiences often take the form of short-term assignments that occur naturally as part of the job like task forces, strategic initiatives, or enterprise-wide projects. Some of the most powerful Broadening experiences described to my research group by leaders involved international assignments. Such experiences are among the most dramatic examples of Broadening because the "differentness" of the experience is unmistakable. One general manager described a particularly valuable international assignment:

> *It was a six-month project where I got to go around Europe doing market research. I went out with all the sales reps. I spent a lot of time on the road really understanding the European market and what we needed to do to be successful there. And that was one of the best experiences I've ever had because I hadn't spent any time outside the U.S. It really broadened my view on things.*

But other types of Broadening experiences were also cited as powerful. For example, one business unit's general manager described his first Broadening assignment as the beginning of his shift from a technical to a business path:

> *I started as a software engineer and moved into being a technical marketing person. That was my first step outside of being a technologist. I liked getting into the marketing side. It just sort of broadened my exposure to how the business worked. Up to that point I had only seen the world from the perspective of somebody who was pounding out code all day.*

Early career individuals can benefit from exposure to a wide range of diverse perspectives. For the early to mid-career individual, Broadening presents an opportunity to develop a better understanding for how other parts of the organization fit together, and an appreciation for the thought processes and challenges that drive others in different functions, organizations, or cultures.

Broadening can be valuable at *any* career stage. Getting exposure to different ways of thinking, other parts of the organization, or different cultures can be invigorating and developmental for anyone. Those who are advanced in their careers can benefit from a range of Broadening experiences, including temporary projects, task teams, international assignments, or boundary-spanning roles. One division President cited a series of valuable Broadening experiences earlier in his career that required him to adapt and learn in a range of areas through very short-term temporary assignments:

> *The new CEO came in and he was taking over with a new vision of things. He wanted someone on the team who understood the business as it had been run, but wasn't too tied to it. So he had a temporary need for me to do some stuff there. And I came in and helped. And he carved out things for me to do—work with this guy on sales and marketing, work on this finance project, etc. It was just incredibly broadening, having this set of temporary assignments for filling specific needs in all these different areas that I didn't really know in any depth.*

Because of the higher stakes involved with senior level leadership responsibilities, at more advanced career stages Broadening can quickly turn into FrameBreaking, which, as we will see, is a riskier type of experience. It is not very common for organizations to intentionally rotate top talent through senior function head or general management roles as Broadening assignments. Most significant leadership roles are filled with the intention of creating Delivering experiences and minimizing risk for the organization.

Common approaches to Broadening

While different individuals will find different experiences more or less Broadening, there are a few approaches that are so widely used as Broadening assignments as to merit mention. These approaches all involve structured settings that put someone into a situation that requires dealing with unfamiliar issues, people, and contexts.

Action learning assignments. Action learning assignments are short-term, single-purpose tasks, typically given to teams formed by bringing together a diverse group of individuals from across the organization and presenting them with a problem to solve. The problems that such teams address are often intentionally selected so as to require exploration across the organization. Teams typically tackle real issues that are outside the scope of the participants' regular jobs. These experiences can be very valuable, but are usually limited to participants in an organization's formal management development program.

Task teams. Most organizations routinely form task teams to address specific, short-term needs. These teams can present opportunities for learning if the need involves grappling with information outside your normal work role or interacting with others from across the organization with differing perspectives from your own.

Job rotation programs. Some organizations use structured programs to rotate employees, generally early in their careers, through a series of diverse functional assignments with the express intent of developing a well-rounded perspective. While these programs can be highly developmental, they have certain limitations that will be described later in this chapter in the section on the Broadening Trap.

Cross-enterprise councils and committees. Councils and committees used to coordinate activities across organizational boundaries can provide participants with Broadening opportunities. These internal service environments can be Broadening because they serve as forums for the consideration of diverse views and perspectives on organizational issues. For example, corporate and divisional perspectives on the design of enterprise-wide processes for managing and developing talent are often discussed through such councils. Understanding such varying perspectives can help you be more effective negotiating on a larger playing field.

External board directorships. Senior executives may gain valuable perspective by participating on another company's board. Outside board memberships can expose an executive to familiar issues that are unfolding in a different context. This type of experience expands one's perspective and ability to spot important patterns in his or her own organization. In addition, the opportunity to interact with board members as equal contributors often involves building relationships with different types of people than you may be used to, interacting with and operating in a context that is unfamiliar.

Leading a virtual team. Leading a virtual team often involves interacting with people who hold different perspectives from your own. Whether they be individuals from different cultures, business units, divisions, departments, or functions, virtual teams frequently require you to relate to other people whose worldview may be new to you. And, if you have not had extensive experience with virtual communications, leading such a team may require you to adapt in new and different ways to accommodate virtual forms of communication.

Volunteer/community work. Volunteer/community settings draw volunteers from all walks of life. As such, they provide opportunities to work with others with very different backgrounds from your own. In addition, you may have the opportunity to tackle problems outside your area of expertise, simply by virtue of being willing to pitch in and do the work. It is not uncommon for an HR manager by day to act as treasurer for a nonprofit or for an IT professional to pitch in on a community organization's marketing campaign.

The Broadening Trap

Given that organizations need to ensure results, most people are not at great risk for getting too many Broadening experiences. It can become a problem, however, when organizations attempt to systematically develop well-rounded leaders through frequent job rotations.

One of the shortcomings of structured job rotation programs is that they risk moving people too quickly through too many assignments. Participants risk missing the opportunity to develop critical skills that will enable them to make their mark. This is referred to as the Broadening Trap (Figure 10). Not only can overly rapid movement inhibit the development of critical skills, it can also result in a missed opportunity to see the long-term impact of one's work—given the nature of

Figure 10.

***Broadening Trap**—Not balancing gaining a broad perspective with the need to develop deep enough skills to have a significant impact*

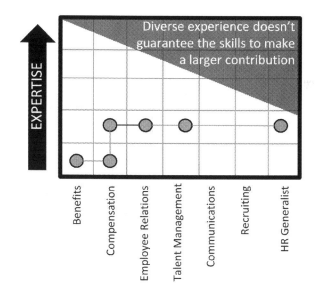

leadership work, the lasting impact of one's effort is generally not discernible within the tenure of a fast-track leader.

Figure 10 depicts the career experiences of a Human Resources professional who is interested in eventually becoming a Chief Human Resource Officer. As depicted here, the individual has had a series of lateral moves, exposing her to various functional areas within HR, including Benefits, Compensation, Employee Relations, and the like. While the breadth of exposure seems attractive on the surface, this individual's problem is that she has not distinguished herself in any particular area. She has contributed at a relatively junior level to work across many of the functional areas within HR, but has not developed enough expertise in any specific area to make a contribution that would showcase her ability to make significant contributions to the organization. When serious promotion opportunities arise, it may be the specialist who has made a significant contribution on a difficult problem that ends up getting the nod.

Should I consider a Broadening experience?

The following questions can help you decide whether a Broadening experience would help you to achieve your career goals.

1) How would a Broadening experience help me to make progress toward my career goal?

   • Do I need to develop broader skills and perspectives in order to achieve my ultimate career goals?

   • Would exposure or limited experience in another organizational area significantly enhance my chances of future success? How?

   • What gaps in my experience would be filled? Are these "must-have" experiences needed for me to achieve my career goal?

2) Would a Broadening experience provide me the opportunity to make a significant contribution to the organization?

   To stay on a steep contribution trajectory, it is important to always consider how your work is contributing to important organizational outcomes. There are times when it may be wise to engage in development activities that do not involve significant results, but you should do so consciously—knowing the trade-offs you are making and why you are making them.

- Is there a way to reshape one of my current performance objectives to make it a Broadening experience?

3) What is the opportunity cost?

Remember that pursuing a Broadening experience would mean not engaging in some other, different, development experience.

- Would learning new things, broadening my perspective, and trying out different types of work be the best way to make progress toward my career goal at this time?

4) Am I passionate about the work I would do in this Broadening experience?

- Do I want different types of experience (different job content or different types of interactions with different types of people) than I have had previously?

- When I think about what it would feel like to do the work I would be doing in a specific Broadening experience, am I motivated and energized?

5) Have I had enough Broadening?

If you repeatedly engage in Broadening experiences, you may find that advancement is slowed because you haven't been in a position to take charge and demonstrate your capabilities through significant achievements.

- Do I need to build my track record with more significant accomplishments? Could I do that while Broadening?

6) Will I have the chance to learn from key leaders?

Often, valuable learning from a Broadening experience comes from interacting with others with whom you would not normally interact. In a Broadening experience, these are likely to be people who share very different perspectives from your own.

When you interact with others with diverse perspectives, seek to learn from them. Try to learn about the goals, motivations, and challenges they face and develop relationships with them. Broadening experiences are an excellent way of expanding your network both inside and outside the organization. Successful leaders often cite the relationships they developed through such experiences as critical to their later success, sometimes in wholly unexpected ways. Long after the experience ends, they are able to call on an extended network and continue to get information on dynamics across the organization because of having a broader set of relationships.

6

Mastering

I had the leadership role in determining the technical product selection, which was about a forty-five million dollar decision. Up until that point in my career, I hadn't even made a million dollar decision, let alone a forty-five million dollar decision... I remember the day of that decision, witnessing the two vendors reactions, positive and negative, and going home and thinking to myself, good God, you just made a forty-five million dollar decision.

- An IT Leader at a large airline

Mastering

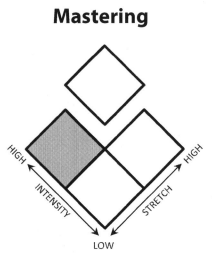

Intensity: Moderate - High

Stretch: Low – Moderate

Individual sees as: "Advancing in my specialty"
- Developing specialized skills and knowledge

- Building on strengths

- Achieving excellence

Organization sees as: *"Building talent in the specialty"*
- Ensuring smooth transitions

- Ensuring a high probability of success

- Maximizing short-term results

- Typical approach: Used to build functional expertise

In a Mastering experience, you deal with situations that involve a higher level of Intensity than you are accustomed to, but within an area that is generally familiar. Although Mastering experiences often involve some degree of Stretch, the learning thrust is primarily related to the Intensity of the experience. Most typically, that Intensity stems from the need to face a significant challenge or solve a difficult problem.

You may be highly motivated to excel in Mastering challenges because they enhance your sense of achievement and self-efficacy. Mastering experiences provide the opportunity to demonstrate your ability to handle larger challenges and achieve more significant results, while also building well-proven skills and knowledge into towering strengths.

Most successful professionals are very familiar with Mastering experiences and will naturally cite them as developmental. After Delivering experiences, these are the types of experiences that organizations feel most comfortable creating for individuals. Many organizations will use Mastering experiences as "proving grounds" for one's ability to perform at a higher level.

Increased opportunities bring increased expectations

As a personal values check, you should make sure that you have thought about what your world would look like if you were *successful* in any significant Mastering experience. Have you given full consideration to both the potential benefits *and* the potential costs of this success? For example, if proving your capabilities were to lead to an advancement opportunity, would you be ready to take on the extra demands it might entail? If the experience could lead to expanded work hours, relocation expectations, more travel, increased pressure from office politics, or other challenges it is a good idea to make sure that you are ready for all that. As you ascend closer to the top of any organization, the demands increase rapidly.

If you will need to make compromises to your personal life, think that through before you go too far. Once you move up the ladder, it may be hard to get back down in one piece. If you back off of opportunities stemming from the larger responsibilities and challenges that the Mastering experience may afford you, it can be interpreted by others as a sign that you "don't have what it takes."

In addition to all of the learning that you will seek, one of the things to ask yourself during a Mastering experience is, "How does it feel to operate on that larger stage?" If, for example, you are taking a bigger leadership role in this activity than you have previously, what might it feel like to be accountable for much more significant decisions? If a lot is at stake, how will you handle the pressure? Are you energized and engaged by the increased responsibility, or are you drained and made anxious by it?

Whenever individuals advance in the hierarchy within their area of specialization, they are going through a Mastering experience. For example, the sales manager who becomes a sales director will generally find the move to be a Mastering experience. Career moves such as these are the expected and predictable advances in responsibilities that many individuals see as career mileposts. Once a specialization is selected, most focus on trying to work their way up into positions with the opportunity to make a greater contribution and have a bigger impact.

It is important to keep in mind that, as with all four of the experience types, Mastering experiences need not involve a job change. In fact, many organizations will provide their people with access to a series of increasingly intense experiences within their area of expertise as a means of preparing them for advancement.

Mastering isn't just for specialists

Because Mastering experiences involve building on knowledge and skills you already possess, these experiences are often associated with specialization and the deepening of pre-existing capabilities. For the specialist, Mastering presents an opportunity to demonstrate capabilities needed to move up within a specialty.

Even so, Mastering can be equally valuable for generalists, whose primary contribution to the organization comes from their ability to combine diverse areas of knowledge and skill. For generalists, the Mastering experience presents an opportunity to build sufficient depth in a key experience area—to acquire an important building block for future success.

For example, the general managers that I spoke with frequently cited the importance of learning to manage salespeople early in their career. Developing a deep understanding of the sales personality, the dynamics of the sales organization, and the effective management of the function is often viewed as providing critical insight to a key piece of the revenue generation puzzle that one eventually needs to solve as a general manager. One publishing leader identified basic sales skills that he learned early in his career as critical to his subsequent success:

> *I've had a pretty interesting set of life experiences that have given me exposure to all of these different perspectives—a small company, a big company, a growing company, business transformation, rationalization, 9/11, and I guess it's the aggregation of all of those experiences that makes me the monster I am today. But probably the most important experience I have had in my career is working as a salesman very early on.*
>
> *Early in my career my job was traipsing around the U.K., France, Switzerland, and Holland selling database products to customers that were asset managers. And the experience of learning how to be a professional salesperson is probably a life experience that benefits you in every aspect of your life forever. Because everything in life is selling, right?*
>
> *Whether it is persuading the customer of the intelligence of doing business with your company versus another, or whether it's going to the people who control the purse strings to persuade them to release some of their valuable assets and resources for something you want to get done, or whether it's to an employee to try and get them to step up to the next level. It's all selling to one degree or another, every interaction we have involves some level of it.*
>
> *Selling is all about understanding where the other person is coming from, figuring out how you can best engage with the other person, and optimizing the chance of getting a*

favorable outcome from that interaction. So it's a foundational skill.

While this executive describes what he learned as a foundational skill, he has clearly integrated this skill into his behavioral repertoire in an advanced fashion. He is not describing a basic sales tactic, but a higher-order insight about the importance of influence as a leader.

The Mastering Trap

The potential risk for individuals who excel in Mastering experiences is to find that they have unintentionally narrowed their career options by becoming a specialist. Figure 11 shows the Mastering Trap. This chart displays the career experiences of an HR professional who has worked his way up through a series of increasingly responsible roles within a narrow band of HR specialty areas. This pattern is typical of individuals who are specialists.

While the specialist path can provide a satisfying and rewarding career, this pattern is portrayed as a "trap" because individuals may find themselves going down this path unintentionally. If the individual has not made a conscious choice to pursue a specialist path, he or she may realize too late that certain desirable options are no longer available.

Figure 11.

Mastering Trap—*Not balancing gaining deep expertise with the need to develop a sufficiently broad skill set and perspective*

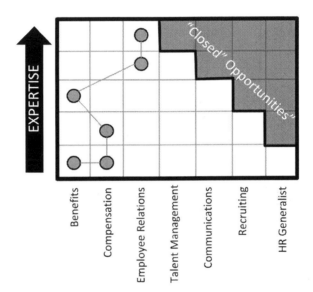

Should I consider a Mastering experience?

The following questions can help you decide whether a Mastering experience would help you to achieve your career goals.

1) How would a Mastering experience help me make progress toward my career goal?

    • Do I need to develop deeper or more advanced skills and perspectives in order to achieve my ultimate career goals?

    • Would bigger, higher-level experience in the same organizational area significantly enhance my chances of future success? How?

    • What gaps in my experience/capabilities would be filled? Are these "must-have" experiences for achieving my career goal?

2) Would a Mastering opportunity provide me the opportunity to make a significant contribution to the organization?

    To stay on a steep contribution trajectory, it is important to always consider how your work is contributing to important organizational outcomes. Mastering generally involves a high level of difficulty within your area of expertise, but does not necessarily mean that you will be making a bigger contribution to the organization.

- Will one of my current performance objectives put me into a Mastering experience? How can I learn from it?

3) What is the opportunity cost?

    Remember that pursuing a Mastering experience would mean not engaging in some other, different development experience.

    - Would deepening my skills and taking on larger responsibilities be the best way to make progress toward my career goal at this time?

4) Am I passionate about the work I would do in a Mastering experience?

    - Do I want the same type of experience (similar job content, similar types of interactions, and similar types of people) as I have had previously?

    - When I think about what it would feel like to do the work I would be doing in a Mastering experience, am I motivated and energized?

5) Have I had enough Mastering?

    If you repeatedly engage in Mastering experiences, you may find that your opportunities are limited because you have developed a narrow skill set.

6) Will I have the chance to learn from key leaders?

Often, valuable learning from a Mastering experience comes from interacting with others in new and different ways. These may be people who share similar perspectives to you, but are at more senior levels or in key positions within the organization.

When you interact with key leaders, seek to learn from them. Try to figure out the good role models for what you want to do and develop relationships with them. Working with a key leader within your area of focus can be a great way to learn in any Mastering experience.

While you may be able to expand your perspective by interacting with more senior leaders and seeing how things operate at a higher level within your specialty, you still may not have the opportunity to gain significantly broadened experience or perspective from a development plan focused on Mastering.

7

FrameBreaking

I was asked to go into this new market and open up a lending operation for the mid-market—five million to fifty million dollar loans. I had the opportunity to decide everything, from what the strategy and marketing plan would be to what the logo would look like. Then, I had to make it all happen—from hiring the people, designing the workspace, working out the prospecting plan. I had some real drudgery jobs over there, like overdraft reporting. Things that I was used to having access to as part of the infrastructure did not exist over there. It was quite fascinating. So I had responsibility for designing a business and then implementing that design. It was an amazing learning experience.

– Senior Vice President, financial services firm

FrameBreaking

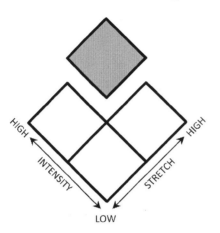

Intensity: High
Stretch: High

Individual sees as: *"Transformational"*
- Changing past ways of thinking

- Challenging assumptions

- Developing new and different skills

- Significant growth opportunity

Organization sees as: *"Sink or swim"*
- Poor person-job fit

- Risk of failure

- Typical approach: Avoid FrameBreaking experiences for development because they are too risky—use them as last resort when there is no other way to get the job done

In a FrameBreaking experience, you deal with situations that involve a higher level of Intensity than you are accustomed to and a situation that is largely new to you. The combination of intense pressure that comes from having responsibility for significant organization outcomes with the need to learn new things outside your prior experience or area of preparation make these experiences transformational. In these experiences, your frame of reference is in some fundamental sense broken and must be re-created with new ways of thinking and acting.

People like to have FrameBreaking experiences...

FrameBreaking experiences may be attractive to individuals because they present the opportunity to take on significantly greater challenges than usual and operate on an expanded playing field. Regardless of what level you are at in your career, having the chance to do something that is high in Intensity and requires you to Stretch in new and different ways can be appealing.

The FrameBreaking experiences that emerged from my research group's work with successful executives were wide-ranging, but, they all had a common theme—the person in the situation was highly engaged and acting at the limit of what they thought they were capable of accomplishing. The FrameBreaking experience was the international leadership assignment to London for a U.S.-bound mid-career professional who wants to be a global executive; the opportunity to launch a new product or offering in a new market; the handling of a crisis situation. While the potential pay-off for successfully navigating FrameBreaking experiences such as these can be substantial, the risk of failure is also substantial. In order to maximize your chances of success, you need to do everything you can to *manage your own transformation.* Understanding that you will need to think differently to be successful can take you a long way toward that success.

...But organizations don't like to put people into FrameBreaking experiences

Some organizations only use FrameBreaking experiences as a last resort, to fill an unexpected opening or need for which no one else is available. One senior leader I worked with described the visceral, lump-in-the-throat fear associated with these risky decisions as "big gulp" moments. For example:

- A strong leader suddenly departs, leaving a large hole, and for lack of a better alternative, a high talent individual from another function is given a FrameBreaking opportunity.

- As a result of a reorganization, spans of control are increased. Some managers go from managing five people to managing 50—*and,* managing a FrameBreaking experience.

Other organizations view what I call FrameBreaking experiences as a form of "trial by fire" or "sink or swim" test of one's talent. Leaders in these organizations often have the attitude of one who has survived a particularly difficult fraternity hazing ritual: "That is what they did to me, so that's what we should do to them." When this is the rationale for the experience, there is an implicit assumption that talented leaders will be successful and "swim." Or, to switch metaphors, the "cream will rise to the top."

Of course, the reality is that many things other than cream rise to the top, and highly talented leaders may sink despite having what it would take to make significantly enhanced contributions to the organization.

The FrameBreaking Trap

Once you are mid-career, any FrameBreaking experiences you have are likely to involve relatively high stakes. The performance demands are high across multiple dimensions (THRIVE), and succeeding will require learning new skills, interacting with people who hold differing perspectives, and perhaps working in a foreign context—business unit, industry, function, or country (REACH).

The primary risk in the most significant FrameBreaking experiences is… everything: failure, burnout, frustration, humiliation, disappointment, job loss, etc. Put simply, the risk is that you will not be able to work your way up the learning curve fast enough to reach the water line before you run out of air (Figure 12). It's called drowning, and the career consequences are significant.

While organizations are more or less tolerant of failed FrameBreaking experiences, you are better off doing what you can to avoid testing your organization's tolerance level.

Figure 12.

FrameBreaking Trap—*Not "sinking" when engaged in a transformational learning experience*

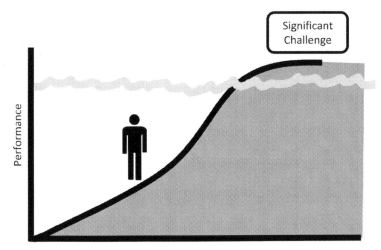

Should I consider a FrameBreaking experience?

The following questions can help you decide whether a FrameBreaking experience would help you achieve your career goals.

1) How would a FrameBreaking experience help me to make progress toward my career goal?

   • Do I need a breakthrough in my personal development or outlook in order to achieve my ultimate career goals?

   • Would a bigger, higher-level experience in a different organizational area significantly enhance my chances of future success? How?

   • What gaps in my experience/capabilities would be filled? Are these "must-have" experiences for me to achieve my career goal?

2) Would a FrameBreaking experience provide me the opportunity to make a significant contribution to the organization?

   To stay on a steep contribution trajectory, it is important to always think about how your work is contributing to important organizational outcomes. FrameBreaking involves a high level of difficulty outside your area of expertise, but does not always mean that you will be making a bigger contribution to the organization.

- Will one of my current performance objectives put me into a FrameBreaking experience? How can I learn from it?

3) Do I really need a FrameBreaking experience?

Each FrameBreaking experience you take on involves an increasing level of risk. After you successfully navigate a FrameBreaking experience, your capabilities expand significantly, it will take even greater challenges and increased Stretch for a future opportunity to be a true FrameBreaking experience for you. As the stakes increase for you, they also increase for the organization. This makes FrameBreaking experiences harder to find as your responsibilities grow. There's also a lot of risk: a single failed FrameBreaking experience at a more senior level can be a serious career setback.

- Would deepening my skills and taking on larger responsibilities be a more effective way to make progress toward my career goal at this time?

- Would broadening my skills and taking on different responsibilities with less at stake be a more effective way to make progress toward my career goal at this time?

4) Am I passionate about the work I would do in this FrameBreaking experience?

- Do I want different types of experiences (different job content, different types of interactions, different types of people) from those I have had previously?

- When I think about what it would feel like to do the work I would be doing in a FrameBreaking experience, am I motivated and energized?

5) Will I have the chance to learn from key leaders?

Often, valuable learning from a FrameBreaking experience comes from interacting with others in new and different ways. These may be people who have different perspectives and are at more senior or key positions within the organization.

- Who are the key people with whom I will interact in this experience? What might I learn from each?

- Who is a good role model for what I want to do? Will this FrameBreaking experience give me an opportunity to develop a relationship with that person as a mentor?

8

Personal Development...
It's not Easy Being Perfect

Think for a moment about what your life would be like if you were completely satisfied with yourself: you always felt fit and energized; you were in your dream job; you were completely happy with your personal and professional relationships; and, you experienced a sense of contentment and inner peace every day. A quick look around (including in the mirror) probably drives home the point that taking yourself from where you are today to where you would like to be on any significant dimension—appearance, skills, attitudes, accomplishments, etc.—is difficult. It must be, or we would have already done it.

107

Before launching into any activity with the intention of improving yourself, it is useful to understand a few basic principles of self-development. Stepping back to reflect on your personal needs and the process of developing yourself can be very helpful in highlighting ways for you to jumpstart your learning and make real, lasting changes in your life. The following five principles of self-development may be helpful to keep in mind as you begin creating your experience-based development plan.

1. Self-awareness is the first step toward self-improvement

Personal development is difficult because most people resist self-awareness. They reach a point where they are pretty comfortable with themselves, and they become resistant to change. A common attitude I have encountered when helping others through personal change is, *"It's worked for me in the past, so why change?"* In order to grow beyond who you are today you must first acknowledge that there is room for improvement.

If you don't have a lot of self-confidence to begin with, focusing on areas for improvement can be pretty threatening. On the other hand, if you have a high level of self-confidence, it is easy to dismiss significant critical feedback. This is one of the major reasons people don't change easily. It's very hard to admit that you need to work on a significant personal change goal. In fact, not only will most people ignore their development needs, many will deny them vehemently when they are pointed out. Recognizing that there is a need for change, then, is the fundamental pre-requisite for making any important change in your life.

So, before beginning a journey of self-development, you need to recognize that you may not like or agree with everything that you encounter along the way. You may find that you are not as good at some things as you thought. If, after understanding your development needs, you decide not to attempt some personal change, at least it's a conscious choice.

2. If you don't know where you're going, you won't know when you get there

It is important to take some time to put your development activities into a larger perspective. What are you trying to develop, what approaches will you take, and how will you know when you have succeeded? You need to approach your personal development with a certain degree of thoughtfulness and planning.

If you allow your development progress to unfold in an *ad hoc* manner, you won't be on the most accelerated path to achieving your goals. On the other hand, if you have a personal development plan—a specific set of needs you are working on over an extended period—it enables you to make better choices about your development and stay on an accelerated course.

3. Structured activity drives out unstructured activity

Someone once suggested that the defining feature of a totalitarian state is that anything not required by the state is prohibited by the state. In other words, all activity is structured, and there is no room whatsoever for individual discretion. When you talk to most people about their personal development, you might think that you were talking to a citizen of a totalitarian state: "My day is so filled with a constant barrage of activity—much of which is driven by the need to respond to others—that I don't have the discretionary time to work on my own development."

The most powerful thing you can do to deal with the demands of an oppressive schedule is impose a little structure on your development agenda. If you create specific goals with action plans and written timelines, you will be more likely to make the time to follow through and improve yourself.

4. Experience is the best teacher

Although the whole point of this book is leveraging experience, this book will not live up to its promise if you don't get out and apply it.

Most people spend less than one tenth of one percent of their work lives in training courses. From that perspective, it is not surprising that you don't learn most of the important things about leadership from a class or a book. However, formal learning, such as the contents of this book, the FrameBreaking website, and the workshops that I teach should be thought of as catalysts for learning. With the right framing, you can get even more out your experiences.

It is worth noting that there can be great value in formal learning programs. As a former professor and Assistant Dean of Executive Education at the University of Minnesota's Carlson School of Management, I am well aware of the significant value formal learning can provide. I have spoken with many, many participants who got great value from their formal learning. In fact, the point throughout this book is that formal learning has its place—and so do other approaches. However, if you were only to turn on your Learning Mindset when engaged in formal learning, you would be setting yourself up for disappointment.

While experience is the best teacher, it can also be the most expensive. The consequences of bumbling your way through some experiences can be high. For example, it may not be best to learn about managing a team on a highly visible project with significant implications for the organization.

5. The more you work at it, the more you'll improve

The fifth and final thing to consider comes from extensive experience working with people engaged in self-development efforts—thousands of individuals in different contexts over many years: *The more you work at it, the more you'll improve.*

If you create a good plan and dedicate some real time to achieving that plan, your effort will have a payoff. You might not see results overnight, but you will make progress.

You might have thrown up your hands in desperation after reading the earlier chapter that described how human perception and the nature of our thought processes tend to limit our ability to learn. If our ability to learn is constrained by our perceptions and fundamental thought processes, what is the point of attempting to get better at learning? It seems hopeless.

But I see it quite differently. Once you know there is an invisible gorilla walking through your professional experiences, you have a much better chance of spotting it. By using the tools available from FrameBreaking.com and applying yourself in an open-minded process of reflection, you can accelerate your development as a leader.

Get started today. You don't need time off from work or anyone's approval to start thinking differently about your experience and getting the most out of it. Break the frame.

Overview of Resources Available from FrameBreaking.com

A comprehensive toolkit

The resources described in the following pages are available for use at FrameBreaking.com. Individual licenses to use the tools are available for purchase online, and organizational licenses can be arranged by contacting Experience-Based Development Associates, LLC through the FrameBreaking.com website.

Five-step process for applying the FrameBreaking Model

I have developed a five-step process to help you use the FrameBreaking model to guide your own development. The process, more completely described in the FrameBreaking Field Guide, consists of five basic steps:

1) Gain insight from your prior experiences and understand your development needs (tool: LearningResumé$_{TM}$)

2) Draft your career theme and development arc (tool: TalentStory$_{TM}$)

3) Identify potential development experiences (*tool:* Experience Assessment)

4) Plan your development (*tool:* Experience-Based Development Plan)

5) Use an ActiveLearning Routine$_{TM}$ to get the most out of your experience (*tool:* ActiveLearning Routine)

The tools used in the FrameBreaking process are briefly described in the following pages.

STEP

1

Gain insight from your prior experiences and understand your development needs

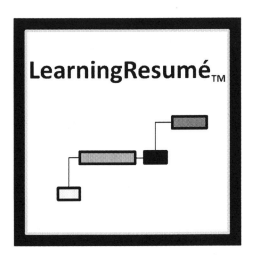

Think of the experiences from your professional career as a stack of case studies on leadership and organizational life—all written about you. The challenges you have faced, your biggest successes, your biggest failures, and the dynamics of your current job. Have you taken the time to read these cases and analyze them to figure out what you did well, or how you might do better?

One of the reasons that we tend not to consciously examine our experiences is that we lack the tools to structure this thought process. And, in the absence of a structured set of tools, we succumb to Gresham's Law, which suggests that "Structured activity drives out unstructured activity." Put differently, unstructured thought and behavior can be mitigated by a conscientious approach.

The LearningResumé is an online tool to help you learn from your past and prepare you to create a robust development plan. Using the LearningResumé, along with the other tools available from FrameBreaking.com, you will answer the following key questions:

- What is my career goal?

- What key experiences have I had throughout my career?

- What have I learned from my experiences?

- What key learning experiences do I still need to achieve my goals?

- What types of experiences should I be seeking?

How it works

The LearningResumé presents a simple interface for entering each of the jobs you have had in your career. As you add each, you are asked to provide a few basic pieces of information:

- Job: Title, Organization, Start/end date

- Responsibilities: Size of budget/P & L managed; # of people within scope of responsibility; Change in responsibilities from prior job (increase, lateral, decrease)

- Key experiences

- Most significant learnings

- Experience Assessment: Your ratings of the experiences using the THRIVE and REACH dimensions from the FrameBreaking model

Using these data, your LearningResumé is generated as a unique visual summary that highlights experiences, learnings, and your career "trajectory." This view can help you to see patterns in your career that you would not otherwise be able to spot.

Sample LearningResumé (actual document in color)

LearningResume

Mark Kizilos
Experience-Based Development Associates, LLC

		Experience	Learning
	$0 0	Creating communications plans for HR initiatives; writing monthly HR newsletter	Basic work ethic and learning how to interact with division ; Understanding of the range of issues dealt with by HR groups
	Community Relations Asst., Honeywell Underseas Systems Division (1987 - 1988)		
	$0 0	Work process redesign for HR department; Coaching engagement with GM of Filter Products	Ability to have real impact on workers lives using my skills; Leading a team of professionals for the first time
	Internship, Rockwell International Semiconductor Products (1988 - 1989)		
	$0 0	Working at corporate headquarters; completing a culture study	Insight into the dynamics at corporate headquarters; Interacting with senior executives and c-suite leaders
	Intern, PepsiCo, Inc. (1989 - 1989)		
	$0 0	Performing various consulting engagements ; Interacting with senior leaders	Contracting with clients for specific deliverables; Performing in the role of expert
	Independent Consultant, Pepsi Cola NA, Taco Bell, Red Lion (1990 - 1994)		
	$0 0	Designing classes for undergraduate students; Living in Canada	Bringing a critical perspective to learning and development; How to create effective learning experiences for classroom
	Assistant Professor, University of Alberta (1995 - 1997)		
	$0 0	Participating in competency modeling studies; Interacting with clients as part of team	Technical knowledge regarding creation of competency models; How to relate to clients as consultant rather than professor
	Consultant, Hay McBer (1997 - 1998)		
	$0 2	Managing client relationships; Creating and selling new product offerings	Importance of relationship building for business success; confidence in ability to create a new offering from scratch
	Principal Consultant, Center for Leadership Solutions (1998 - 2002)		
	$5M - $10M 3	Interacting with senior retail leaders; Creating emerging leaders high potential program	Influence of industry on the nature of leadership challenges; Importance of having direct access to senior exec leaders
	Manager, Organization Capability, CVS/pharmacy (2002 - 2003)		
	$0 2	Creating talent management online system; Developing leadership competency model for company	How to set up, launch, and manage a talent review process ; All aspects of leading change across a global enterprise
	Director, Executive Development, Thomson Corporation (2003 - 2005)		
	$5M - $10M 0	Supporting CEO in talent presentations to Board; Leading talent management organization-wide	executive leadership style and influencing high level group; Influencing others without formal authority
	Vice President, Talent Management, Thomson Corporation (2005 - 2008)		
	$1M - $5M 11 - 20	Managing a profit center and leading in recession; Creating a strategy to realign the business	Leading a multifunction team and keeping team motivated; Innovating a business model
	Assistant Dean, Executive Education, Carlson School of Management (2008 - 2011)		

Arrow	Line Length	Line Color		
Change in responsibility	Years in role	■ =Delivering ▓ =Mastering ▒ =Broadening ■ =FrameBreaking		
▲ =increase ▒ =lateral ▼ =decrease				

My LearningResume 1

119

STEP

2

Draft your career theme and development arc

What's your TalentStory? If you had just five minutes to tell your story to a coach, what would you say?

Do you know how to fit the pieces of your career together to best describe your career trajectory? If you want to make a compelling case to another person in order to get access to the right kinds of development experiences for yourself, you need to engage him or her with a compelling story.

The TalentStory is a tool to help you craft your story. With an understanding of the key experiences and learning from throughout your career this tool will help you to gain deeper insight into your strengths and development needs and prepare you to have a more effective discussion with a coach or mentor.

How it works

The TalentStory is a simple tool that walks you through a structured thought process to create your own TalentStory.

STEP

3

Identify potential development experiences

How much time do you spend planning for a vacation? The answer is probably more than 30 minutes. But how much time do you spend planning before taking on a development experience that could accelerate or derail your career?

Most of us engage in detailed planning when we are deciding how to take a vacation. What will it be like? Will I get enough time for relaxing, energizing, or exploring? Whatever our goals may be for the vacation, we decide on a destination and prepare ourselves to get the most out of it. We bring the "tools" we will need with us.

Surprisingly, we spend much less time planning for experiences that may make or break our professional careers. What might you get out of taking on a challenging new assignment? Serving on a task-force? Leading the launch of a new product? We tend to approach these and other work opportunities with a purely results-oriented lens: Will I be able to perform? What benefits will I get from being successful? We don't spend much time considering *the experience we will have* and how it will help us to develop and learn.

How it works

The Experience Assessment is a simple online tool for evaluating a potential development assignment. Using the FrameBreaking$_{TM}$ model, and the THRIVE and REACH dimensions, you assess the developmental potential of an experience and explore learning and risks to consider *before* engaging in the experience. The online tool creates a customized report to help you maximize the learning from any experience.

STEP

4

Plan your development

The form is the easy part… but you've got to have a form.

Structured activity drives out unstructured activity. While you shouldn't make development planning any harder than it needs to be, you do need to put *some* structure to your development or it will never get done.

One of the most robust findings from the field of psychology in the past 50 years is that setting good goals leads to enhanced performance. Good goals—those that are specific, moderately difficult, and measurable enough that you can get feedback on how you are doing—drive higher performance than vague, "do your best" goals.

The implications of these robust findings for development planning are clear: *get greater clarity about what you are trying to accomplish in your personal development.* What are you trying to learn and how will it help you? If you don't keep answers to these basic questions in mind, you may miss an opportunity to maximize the learning from your development experience.

How it works

The Experience-Based Development Plan is a simple form to structure your development plan.

STEP

5

Use an ActiveLearning Routine to get the most out of your experience

If you don't follow through on an important performance goal, you might lose your job. But if you don't follow through on your development plan, all you stand to lose is a better future.

Most aspiring leaders have a very strong performance drive. In fact, it is so strong that the drive to get results can push everything else—including your own personal growth agenda—to the back burner. If you let personal development considerations simmer on low heat, you may get short term results, but you also may not prepare yourself for a greater future.

But let's be clear. You don't need to sacrifice results to focus on development. You simply need to start adopting an Active Learning Mindset. That means making learning part of how you approach your job—intentionally looking for the learning in significant experiences.

How it Works

The ActiveLearning Routine walks you through a series of questions to uncover insights from your experience that you can apply to be more effective in the future. Suitable for frequent use on the job, the questions can be used to explore the learning in your own experience or to assist another who is seeking to learn from their experience.

References

Arvey, R. D., Rotundo, M., Johnson, W., Zhang, Z., and McGue, M. (2006). *The determinants of leadership role occupancy: Genetic and personality factors.* The Leadership Quarterly, 17, 1–20.

Arvey, R. D., Zhang, Z., Krueger, R., and Avolio, B. (2007). *Developmental and genetic determinants of leadership role occupancy among females.* Journal of Applied Psychology, 92, 693–706.

Bullock, Alan (1999). New Fontana Dictionary of Modern Thought. Harper Collins.

Büssing, André , and Herbig, Britta (2003). *Implicit Knowledge and Experience in Work and Organizations.* International Review of Industrial and Organizational Psychology, 2003, Volume 18, pages 239-280. John Wiley & Sons, Ltd.

Chabris, Christopher and Simmons, Daniel (2010). The Invisible Gorilla: And Other Ways Our Intuitions Deceive Us. Crown Archetype, New York.

Charan, Ram (2005), *Ending the CEO Succession Crisis.* Harvard Business Review, February.

Chemers, Martin M. (2000). *Leadership Research and Theory: A Functional Integration.* Group Dynamics: Theory, Research and Practice, 4:1, 27-43.

Cooper, Cary L. and Argyris, Chris (1998). The Concise Blackwell Encyclopedia of Management. Blackwell Publishers, Ltd.

DeRue, D. Scott and Wellman, Ned (2009). *Developing Leaders via Experience: The Role of Developmental Challenge, Learning Orientation, and Feedback Availability.* Journal of Applied Psychology, 94: 859-875.

DeShon, R. and Gillespie, J.Z. (2005). *A Motivated Action Theory Account of Goal Orientation.* Journal of Applied Psychology, 90, 1096-1127.

Dweck, C.S. (1986). *Motivational Processes Affecting Learning.* American Psychologist, 41, 1040-1048.

Frasier, Colin, Burchell, Brendan, Hay, Dale, and Duveen, Gerard (2004). Introducing Social Psychology. Blackwell Publishers, Ltd.

Gentner, Dedre, Loewenstein, Jeffrey, Thompson, Leigh, and Forbus, Kenneth D. (2009). *Reviving Inert Knowledge: Analogical Abstraction Supports Relational Retrieval of Past Events,* Cognitive Science. Volume 33, Issue 8: pages 1343–1382, November/December 2009.

Lindsey, E. H., Homes, V., and McCall, M. W., Jr. (1987). Key Events in Executives' Lives. Greensboro, NC: Center for Creative Leadership.

Lombardo, Michael M. and Eichinger, Robert W. (2000). *High Potentials as High Learners.* Human Resource Management, 39:4, 321-329.

McCall, M.W., Jr. (2010). *Recasting Leadership Development.* Industrial and Organizational Psychology, 3 (2010), 3–19

McCall, M.W., Jr. (1998). High Flyers: Developing the Next Generation of Leaders. Harvard Business School Press.

McCall, M. W., Jr., and Hollenbeck, G. P. (2002). Developing Global Executives: The Lessons of International Experience. Boston: Harvard Business School Press.

McCall, M. W., Jr., Lombardo, M. M., and Morrison, A. M. (1988). The Lessons of Experience: How Successful Executives Develop on the Job. Lexington, MA: Lexington Books.

McCauley, C., Ruderman, M., Ohlot, P., and Morrow, J. (1994). *Assessing the Developmental Components of Managerial Jobs.* Journal of Applied Psychology, 79:4, 544-560.

McGregor, Jena (2006). *The Struggle to Measure Performance.* Business Week, January 9.

Senge, Peter (1990). The Fifth Discipline: The Art and Practice of the Learning Organization, Doubleday, New York.

Welch, Jack and Byrne, John A. (2001). *Jack Welch: Straight from the Gut.* New York: Warner Books.

Whitehead, Alfred N. (1929). The Aims of Education and Other Essays. New York: The Free Press.

Yost, P., and Plunkett, M. (2009). Real time Leadership Development. London: Blackwell Publishing.

About the Author

Mark Kizilos, Ph.D.
Founder, Experience-Based Development Associates, LLC

Dr. Mark Kizilos is Assistant Dean of Executive Education at the University of Minnesota's Carlson School of Management. His passion for experience-based development has been stoked over a 20-year career as a professor, consultant, and corporate executive. He has led large-scale projects on experience-based leadership development with major corporations, and his talent management work has influenced the careers of thousands of successful leaders.

Kizilos is a frequent speaker on talent management and leadership development and has been a consultant to numerous corporate clients including PepsiCo, Delta Air Lines, Lawson Software, Royal Bank of Canada, WellPoint Health Networks, and Target Corp. Prior to joining the Carlson School, Kizilos was Vice President of Talent Management and the Corporate University for Thomson Corporation (now Thomson Reuters).

Kizilos holds a Ph.D. in Management and Organization from the University of Southern California, a master's degree in Organizational Behavior from Brigham Young University, and a bachelor's degree in Psychology from the University of Minnesota.

Additional Resources
F R A M E B R E A K I N G . C O M

Visit **FrameBreaking.com** for more information about available tools, including:

Live Sessions
- Public Workshops

- Custom/Company Workshops

- Speeches

Online Toolkit
- Subscription access to the online LearningResumé, Experience Assessment tools, and more

Print Materials
- FrameBreaking Leadership Development book

- FrameBreaking Leadership Development Booklet *(36-page version of the book, suitable for use as workshop prework)*

- FrameBreaking Leadership Development Field Guide: *(The print version of the FrameBreaking toolkit suitable for use as a self-paced learning tool; requires online access to use the LearningResumé tool)*

- Sponsor Guide: *(10-page booklet orienting sponsors to the FrameBreaking model and their role in supporting a person's experience–based development)*

Special Prices Available for Certified Coaches